Israel's Nuclear Arsenal

Also of Interest

Arms Control and Defense Postures in the 1980s, edited by Richard Burt

Syria: Modern State in an Ancient Land, John F. Devlin

The Republic of Lebanon: Nation in Jeopardy, David C. Gordon

Jordan: Crossroads of Middle Eastern Events, Peter Gubser

South Yemen: A Marxist Republic in Arabia, Robert W. Stookey

About the Book and Author

Israel's Nuclear Arsenal
Peter Pry

Israel's Nuclear Arsenal is a full inquiry into the likely size and sophistication of the Israeli nuclear weapons program. Among the key questions it addresses are: Did other nations—the United States, France, or West Germany, for example—assist Israel in developing its nuclear weapons capacity? What is the nature of Israel's industrial nuclear infrastructure? What are the design, number, and yield of its atomic bombs? How are they deliverable?

The answers to these queries are important: Israel's nuclear capability is one of the most potentially critical, and least discussed, variables on the world scene today. By providing the most comprehensive and in-depth investigation to date of Israel's atomic military strength, Pry lays the foundation for analyzing Israeli strategic options and the A-bomb's potential to contribute to international stability or instability, war or peace. This book establishes a new basis from which debate over the political and strategic significance of Israeli nuclear arms can proceed.

Peter Pry is presently a graduate student at the University of Southern California, Los Angeles, pursuing a Ph.D. in international relations, specializing in defense and strategic studies. His publications include articles in the *Military Journal, Weapons and Warfare Quarterly,* and *Warship International.*

Israel's Nuclear Arsenal

Peter Pry

Westview Press • Boulder, Colorado

Croom Helm • London, England

This book is included in Westview's Special Studies.

Copyright © 1984 by Westview Press, Inc.

Published in 1984 in the United States of America by Westview Press, Inc., 5500 Central Avenue, Boulder, Colorado 80301; Frederick A. Praeger, Publisher

Published in 1984 in Great Britain by Croom Helm, Ltd., Provident House, Burrell Row, Beckenham, Kent, BR3 1AT

Library of Congress Cataloging in Publication Data
Pry, Peter.
  Israel's nuclear arsenal.
  (A Westview special study)
  Bibliography: p.
  Includes index.
  1. Atomic weapons. 2. Israel—Defenses. I. Title.
U264.P78 1984   355.8′25119′095694   83-23427
ISBN 0-86531-739-9

British Library Cataloguing in Publication Data
Pry, Peter
  Israel's nuclear arsenal.
  1. Atomic weapons 2. Israel—Defences
  I. Title
358′.39′095694   UA853.I8
ISBN 0-7099-2079-2

Printed and bound in the United States of America

10   9   8   7   6   5   4   3   2   1

Contents

Illustrations

Photographs

Introduction

What, specifically, are Israel's atomic weapon capabilities? The answer to this question is not known. Nevertheless, it is vital to U.S. national security to arrive at some conclusions, however tentative, about the strength and configuration of Israel's nuclear arsenal. Many defense experts believe that if another war occurs between the Arabs and the Israelis and the latter were to resort to nuclear force, the United States and the Soviet Union might enter the conflict as well. In their book *Nuclear Threat in the Middle East*, Robert J. Pranger and Dale R. Tahtinen warn that "the chief danger posed for American interests by nuclear war in the Middle East is the possible erosion and rupture in the U.S.-USSR nuclear equilibrium. With this . . . would come a greater probability of nuclear war between the super-powers."[1] Thus, an atomically armed Israel could inadvertently escalate the next Middle Eastern conflict into a global holocaust.

The United States must be able to anticipate what Israel might do with its fission arms in such a scenario and make appropriate contingency plans. In order to assess accurately Israel's nuclear options, before one can judge its strategic capabilities, we must first determine the number, power, range, and other characteristics of that nation's atomic weapons.

Unfortunately, nothing is known for certain about Israel's nuclear forces. Because the Israelis are intentionally ambiguous about their atomic status, we cannot even be sure that an arsenal actually exists. The Israelis desire the security that obtains from a nuclear deterrent, but they refuse to acknowledge its existence, rightly fearing that such a confession might provoke world condemnation and invite international sanctions.

Examples abound of Israel's intentional ambiguity about its status as a nuclear power. In December 1974, President Ephraim Katzir, expressing in deliberately vague language his government's official position on its atomic capabilities, said that Israel would not be the first to introduce nuclear arms into the Middle East, but added that

Israel "has the potential" to construct such devices and could do so "within a reasonable period of time."[2] Katzir's words have been interpreted to mean that Israel has built atomic bombs, or components thereof, but that it has not yet activated or deployed them among its defense forces. The President's remarks suggest that the Israelis stand ready to do so immediately after any deployment of fission or fusion arms by an enemy of Israel.

In a June 1981 interview with *The New York Times*, Moshe Dayan, former Israeli defense and foreign minister, reiterated Katzir's denial that his country possesses atomic arms. But he also said, "We do have the capacity to produce nuclear weapons, and if the Arabs are willing to introduce nuclear weapons into the Middle East, then Israel should not be too late in having nuclear weapons too."[3] Defense analysts widely interpret this statement as a confirmation of the prognosis that Israel possesses semi-ready fission devices that can be made combat-ready on short notice.

More recently, on 2 November 1983 in a conversation with the author former Prime Minister Begin's closest advisor, Shmuel Katz, while being carefully ambiguous reinforced the above conclusion about the existence of semi-ready Israeli A-bombs. Katz denied any "inside" knowledge of Israel's nuclear weapons program, but expressed the opinion that, even if the Arabs were secretly near to completing an atomic device and this became known to Israel, Israel could counter the Arab threat by producing bombs of its own within a few days or less. Such rapid deployment of nuclear weapons by Israel is possible only if bomb components already exist for rapid assembly.[4]

Israel, through numerous high-ranking officials, has acknowledged only that it has "the capacity to produce" atomic arms, but stops short of admitting that it has actually constructed such a weapon.

Despite doubts about Israeli nuclear capabilities, which persist because, so far as is known, the Israelis have never actually detonated an atomic weapon, an enormous body of circumstantial evidence has convinced most military experts that Israel is now a nuclear-armed power. Several authors, notably Fuad Jabber in *Israel and Nuclear Weapons: Present Options and Future Strategies* (1971), have attempted to reconstruct the story of how this country acquired the bomb.[5] Moreover, the Central Intelligence Agency squelched much of the skepticism when, in 1976, it made known its opinion that Israel had manufactured fission armaments.[6]

With a growing agreement about the probable existence of Israel's atomic arsenal, the focus of the controversy has shifted to the question of that arsenal's size and qualities. During the 1970s, numerous articles and books appeared that attempted to define the limits and capabilities of Israeli nuclear might. Many of these works, affected by the strong arguments of Jabber, the 1973 war, and the CIA revelations, almost certainly exaggerated the strength and sophistication of Israel's nuclear arms, particularly as regards delivery systems.[7] Today, enough information has accumulated to make possible some realistic inferences about the nature of Israel's atomic weaponry.

The purpose of my own examination of the issues is twofold. First, it will reconstruct the story of why and how Israel probably developed the A-bomb, a subject long neglected. Most works dealing with the Israeli bomb are mainly concerned with its future strategic and political implications and attempt only superficially or not at all to explain how Israel got the bomb in the first place. The principal scholarly books that analyze in depth the history of Israeli nuclear aspirations are Jabber's (mentioned earlier), to a lesser extent Simha Flapan's "Israel's Attitude Towards the NPT" in *Nuclear Proliferation Problems* (1974), and Robert E. Harkavy's *Spectre of a Middle Eastern Holocaust: The Strategic and Diplomatic Implications of the Israeli Nuclear Weapons Program* (1977). Another book, *None Will Survive Us: The Story of the Israeli A-bomb,* by journalists Ami Dor-On and Eli Teicher, was to have been released in 1980, but it was banned from publication by Israeli government censors. The Dor-On and Teicher manuscript may never become public, as the authors, allegedly threatened with prison sentences of fifteen years to life if they defy the ban, have announced they will respect their government's decision and cease efforts to publish their material.[8]

Histories of the Israeli bomb are few at least in part because of the many uncertainties surrounding the story and the difficulty of obtaining information. The record of Israel's atomic development must be reconstructed largely from secondary sources—newspapers, magazine articles, interviews, and the like—because the government of Israel naturally has classified most documents pertaining to its nuclear program. Jabber's book, now thirteen years old, is still the most detailed and best-documented history of Israel's early atomic efforts.

The bulk of analysis and supposition about Israel's atomic ambitions and capabilities has been published after Jabber's book and much happened after Harkavy's volume. Many fresh hypotheses and facts illuminating the origins of the Israeli A-bomb have surfaced in those studies. Some suggest that the United States was principally responsible for helping Israel acquire fission arms; others point to France or West Germany. Some say Israel uses laser isotope separation (LIS) or gas centrifuges to make uranium weapons, while others argue that hot labs and chemical processes were utilized to manufacture plutonium bombs. Which of these and other theories are most likely correct?

I will discuss the numerous hypotheses, discount those theories that are apparently fanciful, acknowledge the more credible ideas, and attempt to synthesize them into a single history. My objective here is not to duplicate the details already given in Jabber's older history but to paint with broad strokes a portrait of Israel's evolution into a nuclear power, pausing occasionally to deal minutely with controversial issues unaddressed, or addressed inadequately, by earlier works.

The second purpose of my inquiry—and its main objective—is to deduce the basic characteristics of the nuclear arsenal in order to provide a data base for analyzing Israeli strategic options. Strategic options themselves will not be examined. Rather, this study is more narrowly concerned with determining the arsenal's technical features— for example, its A-bomb production capabilities and the number and power of its weapons—so that future works may define possible strategic applications. The term "nuclear arsenal," as used in these pages, refers not only to atomic weaponry—bombs and delivery systems and their characteristics—but also to nuclear production capabilities and industrial and scientific resources, for a nation's capacity to build bombs and to improve its technology is also an important component of its atomic strength.

Like the history of Israel's development of nuclear weapons, analysis of arsenal characteristics has been insufficiently rigorous precisely because so little is known that the subject defies easy penetration. Most authors prefer to speculate about the future strategic implications of an atomic Israel, a mission more glamorous and less difficult than the "nuts and bolts" job of trying to ascertain the present size and shape of Israel's nuclear military machine. Unfortunately, many analyses of the strategic and political implications of the Israeli A-bomb are seriously flawed because of wrong assumptions about the probable characteristics and capabilities of Israel's nuclear arsenal. A realistic assessment of the arsenal's features will provide a foundation for building new, more trustworthy, hypotheses about its implications for the future.

The book is divided into three chapters and a conclusion. Chapter 1 attempts to explain why Israel built the bomb and how it did so. Chapter 2 explores in more technical detail how Israel probably made the A-bomb; describes Israel's scientific and industrial atomic infrastructure; and speculates on the number, power, readiness, and storage location of Israel's fission weapons. Chapter 3 identifies Israel's probable nuclear delivery vehicles.

1
A History of Israel's
Nuclear Weapons Program

Israel's deployment of nuclear weapons would be a natural extension of its historical quest for security. For three decades, ever since 1948 when the United Nations formally acknowledged the sovereignty of Israel, Israeli and Arab have been at war. Outnumbered and under-financed, the Israelis have always fought at a disadvantage. Even today, Israel is an economically troubled, diminutive country of less than 4 million citizens surrounded by oil-rich potential adversaries who—in Syria, Lebanon, Iraq, Iran, and Libya, excluding several other openly hostile nations—have a collective population of some 60 million people. Israel's superior generalship, U.S. military aid, and disunity among the Arab opposition have, until today, compensated for the numerical and economic superiority of the anti-Israeli forces. However, because of the persistent hostility toward Israel on the part of most Middle Eastern states, several of them potentially more powerful than Israel, the long-term future of that nation has always been, and remains today, uncertain. Israel turned to the bomb early in its history to compensate for the great disparity between Arab and Israeli strength, to deter Arab aggression, and to guarantee its own survival.

The Beginning

Israel's nuclear program began at that country's birth. As early as 1948, the Israel Defense Ministry (IDM) sent geologists into the Negev Desert to search for possible sources of uranium. Encouraged by the IDM and Chaim Weizmann, Israel's first president, Israeli universities sent their most promising students abroad the next year to Switzerland, Holland, Britain, and the United States to specialize in atomic studies. Before 1950, the Defense Ministry had established a nuclear research and development branch in the Weizmann Institute at Rehovoth. Staffed by a phalanx of committed physicists, chemists, and engineers, this technical center became the cradle of Israel's atomic science.[1]

Working on their own, the little group at Rehovoth made surprising progress. Exploration of the Negev south of Sidon and Beersheba uncovered vast phosphate deposits containing low-grade uranium. To make possible the recovery of this precious nuclear material, which existed in a diminutive concentration of 100 to 170 parts per million, Weizmann scientists invented new processes for its extraction and refinement. During the first years of the 1950s, Israel Dostrovsky of Weizmann discovered a new way to produce deuterium oxide, or "heavy water," an important moderator in "natural uranium" nuclear reactors that can be used to breed plutonium.[2]

It is unclear whether Israel's early atomic program was, from its inception, intended to create fission weapons, or whether this became its objective only later. At least one authority believes that by 1955, Prime Minister David Ben-Gurion had decided, in response to unrelenting Arab hostility, to begin moving toward a nuclear option. The involvement of the military in the early nuclear effort was implied in 1952, when the Ben-Gurion government secretly founded the Israel Atomic Energy Commission (IAEC) and placed it under the supervision and control of the Defense Ministry. When it was announced in 1954 that the IAEC existed and was affiliated with the military, no one seemed to realize the significance of the event.[3]

The U.S. Connection

The United States unwittingly aided Israel's research on the bomb in 1955, when President Dwight Eisenhower introduced that nation to his "Atoms for Peace" program. This foreign-aid scheme attempted to alleviate the energy problems of developing countries through atomic power and offered participant nations substantial material and technical assistance so that they could master the secrets of nuclear science. Between 1955 and 1960, under the auspices of "Atoms for Peace," fifty-six Israelis received training in the United States Atomic Energy Commission's (USAEC) research centers at the Argonne National Laboratory and at Oak Ridge.[4] Most importantly, in 1955 the U.S. agreed to construct for Israel a 5-megawatt reactor of the light water or "swimming pool" type at Nahal Soreq, near Yavne. (See Figure 1.1.)

The Soreq Nuclear Research Center, home of the Soreq reactor. The reactor dome is pictured here. (*Courtesy Billboard Publications, Inc., 1515 Broadway, New York, NY 10036.*)

The Soreq Reactor

The Eisenhower administration wisely made the sale of the Soreq research reactor, activated on 16 June 1960, contingent upon the institution of certain safeguards so that it could not be used for making arms. Most authorities agree that the small Soreq facility was, and remains, unusable as a possible source of material for Israeli A-bombs. But some authors believe this for the wrong reasons, claiming that Soreq's design prevented, or made prohibitively difficult, any attempt to obtain weapons-grade nuclear fuel.

To some extent, it is true that Soreq's design precludes its use as a source of fission material for atomic bombs. Jabber notes, "Since plutonium is produced from uranium-238, the near absence of this isotope from the fuel of this reactor means that practically no fissile material is being produced."[5] Jabber is right about the disutility of the Soreq reactor for breeding plutonium, but he also implies, incorrectly, that it would be extremely difficult to use the plant to build

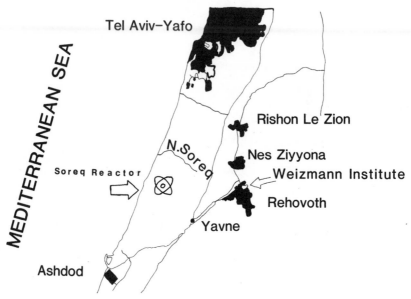

Figure 1.1   Location of the Soreq nuclear reactor and the Weizmann Institute.
The United States provided Israel with its first nuclear reactor, which became
operational in 1960. Soreq, a 5-megawatt research reactor of the "swimming
pool" type, is located on the seacoast between Nahal Soreq and Ashdod, near
the beach west of the town of Yavne. The Weizmann Institute, another atomic
research center, is nearby.

uranium bombs. While he concedes that Israel could "conceivably"
manufacture "3–4 nuclear warheads of the Hiroshima type" from
Soreq uranium, if the Israelis were willing to cannibalize the reactor's
fuel rods, Jabber thinks this would require the construction of enrichment plants to further purify the U-235, which would be technically
impractical.[6] In fact, Soreq can make bombs, and relatively easily.
During the period from 1960 to 1966, the United States agreed to
provide Israel with 50 kilograms of uranium-235, of purity 90%, to
power Soreq.[7] This amount and purity of U-235 are enough, without
further enrichment, to manufacture several fission weapons.

U.S. treaty safeguards, not the technical limitations of the reactor,
were the main reason Israel could not build A-bombs at Soreq. Israel's
agreement with the United States prohibited the use of the facility
for military purposes and allowed the U.S. Atomic Energy Commission
(USAEC) and, later, the International Atomic Energy Agency (IAEA)
to conduct on-site inspections to enforce the agreement's non-military
proviso. Furthermore, Israel was and is still obliged by treaty to
return all of Soreq's spent uranium fuel to the United States, so it

would be extremely difficult to divert U-235 to an arms project.[8] Although U.S. treaty precautions blocked the manufacturing of weapons at the plant, the Soreq reactor gave Israeli scientists invaluable firsthand experience in handling nuclear materials and equipment and prepared them for more ambitious projects.

The "Szulc Thesis"

Aside from the Soreq reactor, just how far U.S. aid to Israel extended, and whether or not it entered the military dimension, is a matter of some controversy. One source charges that under the Eisenhower administration the United States helped Israel develop nuclear weapons. Harkavy notes that in 1975 former *New York Times* reporter Tad Szulc claimed that "the United States government, or elements of it in the CIA [Central Intelligence Agency] acting independently, had given overt assistance to the Israeli nuclear program . . . in the wake of the 1956 Suez war."[9] Szulc implied that "U.S. aid had been given . . . as a quid pro quo for Israel's territorial withdrawals after the 1956 victory and its future cooperation."[10] According to this theory, the 1956 war left President Eisenhower apprehensive about Israel's prospects for survival and determined to provide all possible help in developing an atomic bomb. Purportedly, Eisenhower also wanted to use the promise of nuclear assistance to enhance U.S. influence over Israel. The CIA's alleged technological support allowed Israel to manufacture nuclear weapons in 1957 and 1958 at the Dimona nuclear research center. Szulc claimed that persons close to James Angleton, who headed the counterintelligence staff of the CIA at the time of the alleged nuclear assistance, confirmed his account. The CIA, of course, denies the story.[11]

Twenty-five years have lapsed since Eisenhower supposedly gave Israel the bomb. As yet, no evidence has emerged and no witnesses have come forward to support Szulc's allegations. Moreover, the questions left unanswered raise serious doubts about the credibility of Szulc's story. Why would Eisenhower seek additional, and seemingly unnecessary, political leverage with the Israelis by promising them nuclear weapons when they, then totally dependent upon the West for life-sustaining conventional weapons, were already deeply indebted to the United States?[12] Why would Eisenhower send the CIA to work on nuclear weapons technology at Dimona, a French-built facility staffed with French technicians, when he was opposed to a nuclear-armed France and wanted desperately to keep the A-bomb secret out of French hands? Why would the U.S. help Israel acquire A-bomb technology and then, just three years later, under the Kennedy administration, try to dissuade the Israelis from developing atomic weapons? How could the CIA have helped Israel develop the bomb at Dimona in 1957 and 1958 when this facility was not completed and operational until late 1963?

Most accounts of the origins of Israel's atomic arsenal do not mention, or give short shrift to, the Szulc story. Indeed, Harkavy describes Szulc's charges as "bizarre" and as "wild rumors."[13]

The French Connection

Despite "Atoms for Peace," the Soreq reactor, and the Szulc thesis, it was France, not the United States, that served as Israel's principal mentor in its bid for the bomb. For fourteen years, from 1953 to 1967, first under France's Guy Mollet government and then under Charles de Gaulle, Paris and Tel Aviv worked together secretly on both conventional weapons and nuclear technology.[14]

Three motives apparently lay behind the decision of Mollet and de Gaulle to help their Mediterranean neighbor grow nuclear teeth. First, embroiled in a frustrating war against Algerian rebels, France may have hoped to use the threat of an atomically armed Israel to "coerce" Gamal Nasser and the Egyptians to stop aiding the enemies of French colonialism in Algeria. Second, in order to become militarily independent of the U.S. "nuclear umbrella," France wished to acquire the bomb itself. France exchanged its technical assistance for Israeli "heavy water" and acquired from Israel U.S. computer technology (the United States had prohibited the sale of certain computers to France because of their utility for, and France's obvious interest in, designing A-bombs) as well as the secret of extracting uranium from low-grade ores. Last, before France achieved its first atomic explosion in 1960, it may have viewed French-Israeli nuclear cooperation as an insurance policy against failure to build the bomb. Israel's economic and scientific resources were welcomed into the French missile program, and probably into the nuclear program, as a small but useful reinforcement in the struggle to further France's atomic ambition.[15]

According to Harkavy and William Bader (*The United States and the Spread of Nuclear Weapons*), French-Israeli atomic collaboration became most intimate after Eisenhower's secretary of state, John Foster Dulles, opposed de Gaulle's bid for a special nuclear relationship with the United States parallel to that enjoyed by Great Britain. This rebuff contributed to French estrangement from the North Atlantic Treaty Organization (NATO) in the 1960s and allegedly pushed France closer to Israel.[16]

The opinions of Sylvia Crosbie (*A Tacit Alliance: France and Israel from Suez to the Six Day War*) and Weissman and Krosney run counter to Bader and Harkavy's, who think atomic collaboration between France and Israel peaked in the 1960s. Crosbie seems to accept the word of Jean Renou (formerly of France's Commissariat for Atomic Energy) and Israel's Ernst Bergmann (at one time chairman of the IAEC) "that a braking trend could be discerned after 1959" in French-Israeli nuclear cooperation.[17] Weissmann and Krosney also rely upon the word of French officials that collaboration entered a denouement after 1959. This view is hard to reconcile with the fact that the single most important French-Israeli project—a nuclear reactor in the Negev—was not completed until 1963, with Weissman and Krosney's own allegations of French transfers of data from A-bomb tests during the 1960s, and with Crosbie's own observation that French technicians were still present at Dimona as late as 1969 (1966 according to Weissman and Krosney).[18] In addition to being inconsistent with certain allegations and facts, the view of Renou and Bergmann may be less than objective. Both of these men were representatives of their respective governments and, certainly in Bergmann's case, deeply involved in the atomic exchange. Obviously, they would like to minimize as much as possible the duration and intensity, and hence the importance, of the French-Israeli partnership, especially if its aim was to build atom bombs.

Regardless of whether cooperation peaked before or after 1960, all of the authors mentioned above suggest that the atomic exchange between Israel and France after 1960 remained alive and vigorous. Following the rejection of de Gaulle's overtures to the United States, and after Gallic scientists exploded their first fission device on 13 February 1960, French generals André Beaufre and Pierre Gallois published articles and books advancing the dubious theory that nuclear proliferation could contribute to international stability by making small, vulnerable nations the military equals of their larger neighbors. The appearance of these works was probably timed to vindicate the rise of an atomic France.[19] The writings of Beaufre and Gallois may also have been intended to justify to the United States France's continuing, and perhaps intensified, nuclear cooperation with Israel, which, although supposedly secret, was suspected anyway by the United States.

President John F. Kennedy, in the early 1960s, was probably aware that the Israelis were collaborating with France on atomic weaponry. Later, President Lyndon Johnson offered to sell the Israelis conventional arms, hoping to allay their fears of the Arabs and of their precarious military situation so that they would turn away from the bomb. One author writes, "As the Kennedy administration grew increasingly concerned about nuclear proliferation in general it began to pressure

Israel. . . . This . . . apparently led to the initiation of HAWK-SAM missile sales to Israel as an inducement for it to steer away from nuclear weapons development."[20] However, U.S. efforts to stop French-Israeli nuclear cooperation failed, as is evident from the developments of the 1960s.

During the years of the Gallic-Israeli atomic partnership, Israel acquired the material and scientific resources necessary to become a nuclear power. Israeli engineers and theoretical physicists sharpened their skills in the French atomic research center at Saclay. De Gaulle, whose scientists were conducting detonations from 1960 to 1964 in North Africa, "quite possibly," according to one authority, allowed Israeli scientists access to information from French nuclear blast tests.[21] This last French contribution, if it was in fact made, would be particularly important because, as far as is known, Israel has never performed an atomic detonation test of its own. Perhaps French data provided the Israelis with a blueprint for designing first-generation A-bombs that they could be sure would explode and liberated them from the necessity of doing their own nuclear testing.

The Dimona Reactor

France made its most important nuclear contribution when it sent atomic engineers to Israel to help design and build a 26-megawatt reactor at Dimona. The government of France did not itself construct the reactor, but permitted the nuclear company SGN (Saint-Gobain Nucléaire during the period 1960–1965, currently known as the Société Générale pour le Technique Nouvelle), in which the French government's AEC now owns a 66% controlling interest, to raise Dimona.[22]

Israel's original decision, made in 1957, to acquire the reactor clandestinely was controversial at the highest levels and resulted in the same year in the mass resignation of six of IAEC's seven members, except for Ernst Bergmann, an intimate of the Defense Ministry. The suspicious nature of the Dimona reactor's origins took on an even more sinister aspect a few years later. Around 1961, two of the resigning IAEC scientists helped form the Committee for the Denuclearization of the Israeli-Arab Conflict, an organization of anti-nuclear activists opposed to the introduction of A-bombs into the Middle East.[23] Dimona, which went into operation in December 1963, was capable of producing large amounts of weapons-grade plutonium. Its design was similar to the Savannah River reactors in South Carolina that make Pu-239 for U.S. nuclear bombs.[24]

Significantly, Dimona was a heavy-water reactor that burned natural uranium fuel instead of the enriched uranium used in light-water reactors like the U.S.-built facility near Nahal Soreq. Soreq consumed many kilograms of enriched uranium, which Israel had to purchase from abroad since it lacked the sophisticated facilities necessary to manufacture enriched uranium on a large-scale basis. Because Israel depended upon the United States to provide enriched uranium for its light-water reactor, the United States was able, in exchange for fuel, to prohibit military research at the nuclear plant and to keep its door open for periodic U.S. and U.N. inspections. But the Dimona reactor, which needed only natural uranium fuel that a small nation like Israel could manufacture itself, gave Israel the capability to eventually develop its own fuel sources and thus free itself from U.S. interference with its budding nuclear program. (See Figure 1.2.)

French Motives for Dimona Sale.

As regards French motives for aiding Israel in the construction of the Dimona reactor, Sylvia Crosbie writes, "It was suggested, particularly in the United States, that France needed the Dimona reactor as a source of plutonium for its weapons program, and that Israel would return the plutonium created through irradiation of natural uranium in the reactor core. The Israelis have denied this."[25] Since a public acknowledgment of such an agreement would have absolved both France and Israel of blame for furthering nuclear proliferation, it is probably safe to assume that if Crosbie's plutonium pact existed it was not enforced. The fact that the terms of the Dimona arrangement are still kept secret by both nations does not bode well for the innocence of either party.

Of the rumored French-Israeli plutonium agreement, Jabber says, "Though . . . such stipulations" could have been contained in the original Dimona arrangement, "it is most unlikely that they have been acted upon in view of the marked change in French foreign policy" in the direction of non-cooperation, "which has been particularly manifest in the armaments field and had already set in by the time Dimona reactor produced its first plutonium yield."[26] Jabber also thinks that if an agreement existed calling for the Israelis to return Dimona's plutonium to France for separation, they would have received back part or all of Dimona's produce, "in which case Israel would be in possession of a stockpile of weapons-grade separated plutonium."[27] Weissman and Krosney claim that during interviews two unidentified former officials of the Israeli and French atomic programs confirmed to them that, as Jabber suspects, the Dimona contract required France to separate Dimona's plutonium and ship it back to Israel. According to Weissman and Krosney, their Israeli source acknowledges that such an agreement existed, but denies that France honored it. Their anonymous French source, however, alleges

14

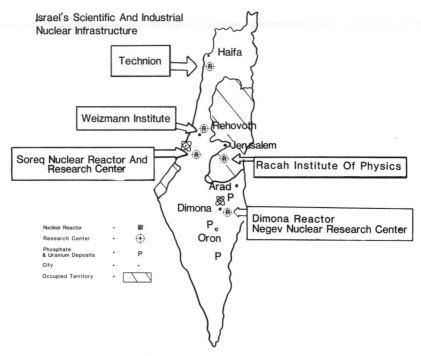

Israel's Scientific And Industrial Nuclear Infrastructure

Technion

Haifa

Weizmann Institute

Rehovoth

Jerusalem

Soreq Nuclear Reactor And Research Center

Racah Institute Of Physics

Arad

Dimona

P

P

Oron

Dimona Reactor Negev Nuclear Research Center

Nuclear Reactor

Research Center

Phosphate & Uranium Deposits

City

Occupied Territory

Figure 1.2   Israel's scientific and industrial nuclear infrastructure. The map shows the location of Israel's main atomic research institutions, reactors, and domestic sources of raw material for reactor fuel and, perhaps, for fission weapons. Israel has three major university institutions that train atomic physicists and engineers: the Weizmann Institute of Science at Rehovoth, Racah Institute of Physics at Hebrew University of Jerusalem, and Technion, Israel Institute of Technology in Haifa. Of these, the Weizmann Institute is the largest, with the most advanced atomic research equipment. The university institutions and the Soreq Center probably conduct peaceful nuclear research only.

The Soreq and Dimona reactors are Israel's most important research and development facilities. The Israeli government, through its Atomic Energy Commission, which is headed by the prime minister, controls the Soreq Nuclear Research Center and the Negev Nuclear Research Center and their reactors.

The Negev Nuclear Research Center, located in the desert near the town of Dimona, is the most advanced atomic research institute and home of the most powerful reactor. The center is situated in the middle of Israel's vast phosphate deposits, which contain 25,000 tons of proven uranium reserves, and facilities for mining phosphates and extracting natural uranium are located close by, in the vicinity of Arad and Oron. The Negev Center may be where Israel's atomic bombs are built and stored.

that in 1967 Israel sent France 40 tons of Dimona's spent fuel, rich with plutonium, and that French technicians separated and returned "about half" or enough for "fifteen to twenty bombs."[28]

In exchange for Dimona, Israel most likely paid cash (reportedly about $130 million) and provided France with secret atomic information (specifically, the Israeli method of manufacturing heavy water and extracting uranium from low-grade sources).[29] Crosbie's implication that Israel gave up all of Dimona's plutonium lacks credibility, since it needed this material for its own atomic project. If the Israelis did surrender Dimona's plutonium, they would, in essence, have been giving up large sums of money and all of their nuclear knowledge to France, receiving nothing in return.

Inspections of the Dimona Reactor.

The Dimona reactor became home for the Negev Nuclear Research Center, Israel's main atomic science institute and, it is believed, the focal point of most Israeli atomic activities.[30] France made no provisions for inspecting the reactor, either with its own people or with IAEA officials, to prevent its use for military purposes.[31] The United States, however, apprehensive about the new reactor, was able to use its influence to win inspection rights, though evidently very limited and inadequate ones.

George Quester, in "Implications of SALT Outcome for Potential 'Nth' Powers: Israel, India, and Others," wrote at the time of the inspections, "the U.S. has demanded and received the right to 'visit' Dimona twice a year, although these are not to be labeled officially as inspections."[32] Jabber repeats this information, while Harkavy says that "during the 1960s, U.S. pressures also apparently led to the regulation of periodic 'inspections' of Dimona. . . . The inspections are now widely assumed to have been casual and perfunctory and to have petered out altogether in a few years."[33] The 1969 inspection team complained in writing that because the Israelis made their earlier inspections hurried and limited and did not permit them to move about freely, they could not guarantee that there was no weapons-related work being done at Dimona.[34]

Evidently in another attempt to pry the Negev Nuclear Research Center open, during the late 1960s, the United States proposed to give Israel technical assistance and $40 million toward the construction of a nuclear desalination plant, contingent upon Israel's submitting the Dimona reactor to international safeguards. Israel refused the offer. In the words of General D. K. Palit and P.K.S. Namboodiri (*Pakistan's Islamic Bomb*), "The fact that the Israelis rejected the plant, which . . . could have been highly beneficial to the country's economy, is indicative of what they proposed to do with their atomic energy establishments at Dimona."[35]

After 1969, Israel disallowed even limited inspections.[36] Ernest W. Lefever (*Nuclear Arms in the Third World*) writes, "a U.S. congressional inquiry" of 1974 "into Israeli and Egyptian nuclear efforts complained of the lack of 'any detailed knowledge by the United States of the purpose, research, and experiments conducted at the Dimona research facility.' In November 1976, thirteen U.S. senators on a nuclear fact-finding tour of the Middle East were barred from the facility."[37] The preceding facts make clear that when France turned on the Dimona reactor in late 1963, Israel gained atomic independence from the United States. Dimona enabled the Israelis to close the door of their most important laboratory to U.S. inspections and, presumably, to proceed with their work on the bomb unobserved.

French-Israeli A-bomb Collaboration

Some sources speculate that France made a nuclear contribution even more important than Dimona. It is possible that from 1960 to 1964, France may have helped the Israelis design and detonate their own first experimental A-bomb at its Reggan or Ekker proving grounds in Algeria.[38] But there is no proof of such a test; indeed, there is reason to believe that Israel's alleged Algerian nuclear experiment never occurred. The Israelis could not obtain from their reactor enough fissionable material for bomb construction until after 1965—too late for the purported Algerian test, since France dismantled its Reggan atomic site in 1964 and conducted no more Saharan detonations thereafter.[39] Harkavy speculates that perhaps France gave Israel enough plutonium or uranium to build a nuclear weapon.[40] But this also is doubtful, as the French were themselves intent on building and testing bombs (they detonated four devices, one of 70 kilotons, in the fourteen-month period from 13 February 1960 to 25 April 1961 alone) and must have needed virtually all of their fission fuel to support their own ambitious weapons program.[41]

Weissman and Krosney claim positive knowledge that Israel profited from French nuclear testing, not necessarily by participating directly in the experiments but because Israeli scientists received critical French test data on A-bomb design and performance. The authors assert that France shared this sensitive information in exchange for aid from Israeli scientists in building France's first bomb:

> The key to the aid was this: Israeli scientists were already making startling advances in weaponry, especially in guidance-control mechanisms perfected in the early 1960s in the Israeli-invented Shavit and

Jericho missile systems. Now some Israeli scientists turned their attention to the design of the French nuclear weapon, and played a leading role in its planning and development. (This aid, revealed to us by an American source, has been denied, we should add, both in Jerusalem and Paris. But we believe it to be true.) That would make the *force de frappe* a very kosher weapon, and the French were obligated to offer the Israelis a substantial quid pro quo.[42]

Weissman and Krosney say that, in exchange for this aid, France gave Israel the Dimona reactor, "a starting hand in building a small facility to reprocess plutonium from spent reactor fuel," and, most importantly, "unrestricted access to the French nuclear test explosion data."[43] If true, these last French concessions would be even more instrumental than the Dimona reactor in furthering Israel's A-bomb program. But is it true?

Weismann and Krosney's source makes misleading suggestions and factual errors that injure his credibility. The source implies that Israeli rocketry so impressed the French that, in exchange for Israel's superior missile expertise, they invited Israeli scientists to help "design . . . the French nuclear weapon," as if French scientists lacked the sophistication to undertake this project on their own. It is misleading to suggest that its "startling advances in weaponry" of the early 1960s placed Israel on a technological par with France, or with any other great power. Although Israel's scientific military progress was very impressive for a nation of its small size, its tank, aircraft, rocket, electrical, and chemical industries were then only in a seminal stage and depended heavily for complex hardware upon imports from France, which had a much larger and more advanced scientific and industrial base.

Israel may have been superior to France in some specific aspects of missile technology. The Israelis had access to U.S. computers, unavailable to France, that could have been useful in the manufacture of liquid fuel, and their solid fuel technology was more advanced, at least according to the Israelis.[44] French missile expertise compared to Israel's, however, has always been superior overall. France built and tested rockets before Israel and has always maintained a missile inventory more numerous, varied, and sophisticated. During the early 1960s Israel reportedly paid France $100 million to help develop the Jericho, Israel's most advanced rocket, thereby implicitly acknowledging France's superiority in rocket engineering.[45] In any joint French-Israeli venture into military research, including missile or atomic research, Israel would certainly be the junior partner and learn more from France than it taught in return.

This raises a key question: What technology could Israel sell to France that was so valuable, so far beyond the latter's reach, that France would be willing to purchase it at the price of the A-bomb secret? It has already been noted that France was interested in Israel's methods of manufacturing deuterium oxide and obtaining uranium from low-grade phosphate ore, as well as embargoed American computer technology then possessed by Israel. France's building of the Dimona reactor, however, seems more than sufficient compensation for all of these items. The suggestion made by Weissman and Krosney's source, that France shared its nuclear test data as a "quid pro quo" for Israel's "startling advances in weaponry, especially in guidance control mechanisms perfected in . . . the Israeli invented Shavit and Jericho missile systems," is unconvincing. First, it is misleading to describe the Israeli guidance-control mechanisms for Shavit and Jericho as "startling advances." Though impressive inventions for a small nation, these systems were not exceptionally precise, even by the inaccurate standards of rocketry during the early 1960s. Next, it is incorrect to classify the original Shavit as "weaponry," since it was only a meteorological sounding rocket.[46] Finally, Shavit probably is not "Israeli-invented" and Jericho certainly is not—both systems seem to have been developed jointly by Israel and France. Crosbie writes "while the Israelis maintain that Shavit was purely a local product, they probably received some technical advice from France."[47] Indeed, France's contribution to Shavit may well have been critical since it had tested similar missiles in the Sahara in the presence of Israeli observers.[48] In the case of Jericho, France can arguably be given the lion's share of credit for the invention of this, by far the larger and more important of the two missiles, as it was first constructed in French factories and launched by French scientists at their Algeria and Toulon test sites.[49] Consequently, it is quite unbelievable that France would share its nuclear test data with Israel in exchange for help on rocket projects to which France contributed at least equally and of which Israel was the primary beneficiary (Israel, not France, ultimately adopted Shavit and Jericho as part of its missile inventory).

Given what we know about French-Israeli nuclear collaboration, the allegation that France allowed Israel to participate in its A-bomb project and to have access to test data may well be true. But Weissman and Krosney's source (who is American, not French or Israeli, so he may be only guessing) makes too many mistakes to be really persuasive, and anonymity does not enhance credibility.

France's single most significant known contribution to Israeli atomic science, then, was the construction of the nuclear reactor at Dimona. Once the Dimona reactor began yielding Pu-239, one of the three major technical obstacles standing between Israel and the bomb was overcome. Israel now had the means to manufacture large quantities of plutonium for atomic arms. In 1966, the Israelis may have been very close to developing nuclear weapons, for, as if in recognition of the Israel Atomic Energy Commission's soon-to-be-realized military importance, the IAEC was reorganized and placed under the direct command of the prime minister, who became its head.[50] Events that occurred the very next year gave Israel an immediate, compelling motive for carrying its atomic project to completion.

The Decision to Build Nuclear Weapons

Israel probably made the awesome decision to construct nuclear weapons in the aftermath of the 1967 Six Day War. Despite its resounding victory in that conflict, the post-bellum diplomatic and military situation left Israeli leaders profoundly insecure. At the war's onset, France abandoned them. De Gaulle, desiring to rejuvenate his strained relations with oil-rich Arabs and under pressure from the United States to end nuclear collaboration with Israel, severed all military ties with the embattled nation.[51] After the 1967 conflict, while France imposed an arms embargo upon Israel, Syria and Egypt received massive new shipments of tanks, jets, and small arms from the Soviet Union. Pressures from the United States at this time in connection with Phantom jet sales may have made the Israelis question the reliability of the United States and probably contributed to their feeling of isolation. The wartime capture of Egyptian nerve gas, in addition to the knowledge that Egypt used gas when fighting in Yemen, raised fears in some quarters that the Arabs might in the future wage a genocidal chemical campaign against Israel.[52] According to Israeli military expert Avidgor Haselkorn (in Harkavy's words), following the 1967 conflict "the 'holocaust syndrome' became a more vivid and imminent reality to Israeli decision-makers and fears of a Soviet preemptive strike on Dimona to crush the nascent nuclear weapons program loomed large in their thinking."[53] Surrounded by seemingly implacable enemies and almost entirely dependent upon the United States for military hardware, Israeli leaders apparently were haunted by doubts about the ability of their nation to survive another war.

As alleged by most accounts, amidst this uncertainty the Israelis turned for security to the power of the bomb. The decision to take the final steps to produce nuclear weapons—constructing a plutonium separation plant (SP) for actual building of the bombs—evidently was controversial. The *Time* article "How Israel Got the Bomb" (12 April 1976), supposedly based on information from a high-ranking

A

B

C

Architects of Israel's nuclear policy. Prime Minister David Ben-Gurion (A) apparently decided during the early 1950s to develop an Israeli atomic option. He forged a nuclear relationship with France, built the Soreq and Dimona reactors, and tried to keep Dimona's existence secret. Following the Six Day War, Defense Minister Moshe Dayan (B) and Deputy Defense Minister Shimon Peres allegedly advocated construction of a separation plant to be used for building A-bombs. Golda Meir (C), Israel's premier when its first bombs were probably completed during the period from 1969 to 1973, purportedly considered using the bomb in the October War. Prime Minister Menachem Begin ordered the Israeli air force to destroy Iraq's Osirak reactor in 1981, demonstrating his government's determination to prevent the Arab nations from acquiring atomic arms. (*Photos courtesy of David Rubinger,* Time Magazine.)

Israeli official, reports that after "an intense secret debate," the "Israeli equivalent of the U.S. National Security Council," led by A-bomb opponents Premier Levi Eshkol, Mapai leader Golda Meir, and Cabinet Defense Committee member Yigal Allon, "vetoed the separation plant project in early 1968." However, "Shortly afterward, Eshkol discovered that Dayan . . . had secretly ordered the start of construction on an SP. Eshkol and his advisors felt that they could only rubberstamp a project already underway." Thus, *Time* asserts that the Israel Defense Ministry set its scientists to work on the bomb "in the wake of the 1967 . . . war."[54]

Whether *Time*'s story is accurate is impossible to say. The allegation that Moshe Dayan had the nerve to order construction of an SP unilaterally, in the face of so much political opposition, including that of the prime minister himself, seems incredible. For all that, *Time*'s is the only account that claims to rise above sheer conjecture, that claims positive knowledge of the details of Israel's decision to take the final steps toward the bomb. Moreover, the account is chronologically consistent with Israel's known capabilities. By 1967 Dimona should have produced enough plutonium for weapons, so the question of whether or not to proceed, it seems, ought to have arisen at this time. Interestingly, consistent with *Time*'s claim about when Israel decided to build the bomb, after the Six Day War on 14 June 1967 *The New York Times* reported that "Authoritative sources" (presumably Israeli government officials) "in Tel Aviv" said "that Israel's next move may be to make the atom bomb."[55] Israeli army censors tried to spike this item.[56]

A-bomb Construction

In order to build an atomic bomb, the Israelis had to overcome several obstacles. The need for a reactor for manufacturing plutonium had been met when Dimona went into operation in late 1963. Two other technical hurdles remained—the need for natural uranium for fueling the reactor and for conversion into plutonium, and the need for a separation plant, or access to another nation's separation facilities, to refine the plutonium into weapons-grade material. A less critical concern was securing the financing for the A-bomb's construction.

Financing the Bomb

Nuclear experts affiliated with the United Nations estimate the total cost of a modest plutonium bomb program, capable of producing ten Nagasaki-sized bombs over a ten-year period, is about $104

TABLE 1.1.   The Economics of Israeli Nuclear Weapons Development: Alternative
Funding Sources and the Financial Impact of A-bomb Construction, 1969-1973

Israel's Average Annual GNP, Defense, and Military Research and Development Budgets for 1969-1973 (in millions of U.S.$)	Average Annual Cost of Building One Nagasaki-Sized A-bomb per Year (in millions of U.S.$)	Annual Cost of A-bomb Program as Percentage of Budget
Gross national product: 6700	10.4	0.16
Defense budget: 1600	10.4	0.65
Military research and development: 67	10.4	16.00

Sources: Data on Israel's GNP and defense expenditures for the period
from 1969 to 1973 can be found in issues of The Military Balance (London:
International Institute for Strategic Studies) for the relevant years.   Report
of the Secretary General (U Thant), The Effects of the Possible Use of Nuclear
Weapons and on the Security and Economic Implications for States of the
Acquisition and Further Development of These Weapons (New York: United
Nations, Department of Political and Security Council Affairs, 1968), p. 61.
Todd Friedman, "Israel's Nuclear Option," Bulletin of the Atomic Scientists,
Vol. 30 (September 1974), p. 33.   Trevor N. Dupuy, Grace P. Hayes, John A. C.
Andrews, The Almanac of World Military Power (London and New York: R. R.
Bowker, 1974), p. 182.

million. Thus, the annual cost of building one bomb per year would
be $10.4 million.[57] Israel could easily afford to spend this amount.

During the period from 1969 to 1973, when Israel is believed to
have built its first bombs, its gross national product (GNP) averaged
$6.7 billion annually, so the cost of an A-bomb project would have
absorbed only 0.16% of the GNP every year. From 1969 to 1973 the
Israelis spent, on average, $1.6 billion annually on defense. A nuclear
weapons project costing $10.4 million would have diverted less than
1% of the defense budget. Israel annually spends about 1% of its
GNP on military research and development (R&D)—which amounted
to an average yearly outlay of $67 million from 1969 to 1973.[58] A
$10.4 million dollar A-bomb project would have cost 16% of Israeli
R&D funds every year. Israel's expenditures on defense and military
research and development rose in the years after 1973, so an A-bomb
project has become increasingly affordable. (See Table 1.1.) These
expenditures are minimal and easily affordable for a nation that
believes its survival requires the guarantee of the ultimate weapon.
Obviously, financing an A-bomb posed no problem to Israel. Securing
the technological means for constructing nuclear arms must have been
a more intractable matter.

Fueling the Dimona Reactor

Fueling was a problem when the Dimona reactor was first activated and probably continued to trouble Israel's nuclear weapons program after 1967. In order to draw plutonium from Dimona, the plant required 24 tons of natural uranium yearly.[59] During the mid-1960s, Israel could manufacture, as a byproduct of its phosphate industry, 10 tons of uranium yearly, leaving it 14 tons short of the amount needed to run Dimona.[60]

The Israelis solved the problem of feeding their reactor by supplementing their own inadequate uranium production with ore from foreign sources. Dimona's first fuel charge (1963) reportedly came from Israel's domestic production (10 tons), from South Africa (10 tons), and the remainder from France.[61] French uranium sales to Israel, however, may have ceased altogether after the break between the two countries in 1967. Israel allegedly received later uranium fuel charges from South Africa, Argentina, and possibly Brazil (an Israeli-Brazilian nuclear cooperation agreement was concluded in 1967). Other countries that were possible uranium sources include Canada, Gabon, the Congo, Central African Republic, and Niger.[62]

After the break with France, uranium for Dimona may also have come from an elaborate Israeli clandestine operation, convincingly described in the book *The Plumbat Affair*, which alleges that Israel illegally obtained from Belgium the fuel needed to run its reactor. The target of the Israeli operation was "yellow cake," (uranium oxide) stored in Antwerp, which belonged to the Société Générale de Belgique. The Société Générale's uranium fuel was available for sale to other nations but not to Israel, since EURATOM—the Common Market nuclear regulatory agency—forbade transfers of such material to Israel because of Dimona's uninspected status. According to *The Plumbat Affair*, in order to deceive EURATOM, Israel paid a West German chemical firm, Asmara Chemie, to serve as a "front" company. Asmara purchased the Société Générale's "yellow cake" in 1968. To discretely move the uranium oxide out of Europe, the Israelis purchased a West German freighter, the *Scheersberg A*, manned it with an international crew, and loaded the uranium aboard in drums marked "plumbat." Through Asmara Chemie, they secured EURATOM's permission to ship the nuclear cargo through the Mediterranean to Genoa for special processing.

Scheersberg A and its load of "plumbat" never reached Genoa. The authors of *The Plumbat Affair* believe that just after midnight on 17 November 1968, somewhere between Cyprus and Turkey, the ship transferred its cargo to an Israeli freighter. *Scheersberg A* went on to the Turkish port of Iskenderun, where it took on a new captain and crew, and sailed shortly thereafter into the center of an international controversy as EURATOM authorities became aware of its mysterious movements and of the disappearance of the "yellow cake." The Israeli freighter, reportedly loaded with "yellow cake," returned home. If the story told in *The Plumbat Affair* is true, and the evidence presented therein is persuasive, Israel obtained in this 1968 operation some 200 tons of uranium oxide, enough to feed the Dimona reactor for about eight years.[63]

According to nuclear expert Nicholas Valéry ("Israel's Silent Gamble with the Bomb," *New Scientist*), by 1972 'srael had freed itself from dependence on foreign uranium imports and presumably from the necessity of "plumbat-type" operations. From the Negev's 25,000 tons of proven reserves, located in and around the Efe and Zefa valleys, Israel mining industries began extracting yearly 40 to 50 tons of uranium oxide, or double Dimona's annual fuel requirements, according to Valéry.[64] But Crosbie claims that as of 1974, Israel still relied on uranium imports to feed Dimona because "refining uranium from phosphates costs as much as ten times more per ton than does uranium on the world market."[65] Todd Friedman ("Israel's Nuclear Option," *Bulletin of the Atomic Scientists*) agrees that Israel was not yet uranium-independent in 1974, but writes, "Israel could soon be self-sufficient in natural uranium supplies and could in the near future produce about 90 tons of uranium a year."[66] (Friedman made this prediction ten years ago, so if Valéry was wrong about Israel's being self-sufficient in 1972, Israel now may well be uranium-independent.)

The balance of expert opinion is that during the critical period after 1967 (when Israel was almost certainly trying to develop its first nuclear weapons) until 1973 (the latest date given by any author for the completion of the first A-bomb), Israel was not self-sufficient in natural uranium fuel for Dimona. The Israelis probably overcame the fuel "stumbling block" both by extracting uranium from their own Negev deposits and by importing it, legally and clandestinely. They managed to feed the Dimona reactor and, apparently, to keep it constantly running to breed plutonium. By the end of the sixties, Israel must have had the raw material necessary for becoming a nuclear power.

Plutonium Separation

Probably sometime in the late 1960s, when Dimona's cumulative plutonium yield was sufficient for several bombs, the Israelis attacked the last major technical obstacle to the fulfillment of their atomic aspirations: separation of the Pu-239. How Israeli scientists converted raw plutonium into weapons-grade material is unknown. The major nuclear powers perform this operation in a chemical separation complex. Jabber concludes that Israel has "traveled all the stages" along the road toward the bomb "except the last: apparently, a chemical separation plant has not been built."[67] He bases this judgment on the fact that an Israeli SP has not been spotted and on the assumption that "these plants are very difficult to dissimulate" because their vast size and "typical long, tall, windowless shape . . . and other characteristic features will give them easily away" to satellites and spy-planes.[68] But he also mentions that former USAEC chairman Glenn Seaborg has asserted that "it is not impossible to construct" an SP "in secret, particularly if it is designed to handle small quantities of spent fuel."[69]

Leonard Beaton ("Why Israel Does Not Need the Bomb," *New Middle East*) thinks a large-scale SP is not essential to bomb construction and that separation of weapons-grade plutonium can be done in the hot labs now existing at Soreq and Dimona.[70] Crosbie suggests that French-Israeli nuclear cooperation continued, presumably on a subdued level, until 1969, as even at that late date "French technicians" were seen "at the Dimona installation."[71] Perhaps Dimona's plutonium circulated through French separation facilities.

Then again, many authorities think that the Israelis do possess an SP after all or some kind of technology for separating plutonium. A German magazine, *Der Spiegel,* reports that Israel does indeed possess a plutonium SP.[72] Weissman and Krosney believe Israel can separate plutonium.[73] Friedman doubts the existence of a large scale SP but, like Beaton, believes that Israel can perform plutonium separation and "could develop nuclear weapons using only its existing facilities, that is, its hot laboratories" at Soreq and Dimona.[74] Lefever claims that "there are large scale facilities for separating weapons-grade plutonium from spent fuel at the Soreq research establishment at Dimona."[75] *Time* tells us that, according to some Western intelligence reports, Israel completed its SP in 1969.[76] The CIA, in a secret briefing to the Nuclear Regulatory Commission in 1976, expressed the opinion that Israel was somehow separating Dimona plutonium to bomb quality. Finally, most ominously, Francis Perrin, former chief of the French Atomic Energy Commission, admits that during the years when Dimona was being erected, France "also participated in the building of a plutonium extraction plant."[77]

Uranium Enrichment

Another theory, one that assumes Israeli bombs use uranium-235 and not plutonium for fission, contends that IDM scientists perfected a laser isotope separation (LIS) technique.[78] It is theoretically possible to remove all the U-235 from natural uranium by means of laser enrichment of uranium isotopes, at a significant savings in the size and cost of enrichment facilities. Unlike gaseous diffusion works, an LIS plant for uranium refinement could be small and easily concealed. The CIA at one time suspected that Isaiah Nebenzahl, a physicist with Israel's Ministry of Defense, and Menahem Levin, of Tel Aviv University, might have made a scientific breakthrough in laser isotope separation.[79] This supposition was largely based on an abstract written by Nebenzahl and Levin claiming that, in twenty-four hours, their LIS technique produced a yield of 7 grams of uranium-235 of purity 60%. One weapons authority observes that a clever designer would need about 50 kilograms of uranium enriched to 60% U-235 to make a fission bomb.[80] But most nuclear weapons experts doubt that Israel yet possesses an LIS capability applicable to bomb production. Robert Gillette, for example, in his article "Uranium Enrichment: Rumors of Israeli Progress with Lasers" (*Science*), concludes that "no one is yet lasing natural uranium into gram lots of bomb quality material."[81] Mason Willrich and Theodore Taylor, in *Nuclear Theft*, express the opinion that "for at least a few more years" the LIS technique "will be extremely costly and complex and probably beyond the reach of any but the highly industrialized nations."[82] Gillette, Willrich, and Taylor are probably right. Since both France and the United States worked unsuccessfully for years on LIS, this technology is almost certainly far beyond the reach of Israel.

Yet another theory, which also assumes the bombs use U-235 and not Pu-239 for fission fuel, suggests that Israel's engineers enrich uranium using gas centrifuges. Like an LIS plant, a centrifuge separation complex would be small enough to hide in the hot labs at Soreq and Dimona. Unlike LIS, centrifuge plants are practical— centrifuges are now operating commercially in the United Kingdom and the Netherlands.[83] This technology is, in Harkavy's words, "unlikely" for the Israelis "but certainly not impossible" and may be within their grasp.[84]

Nevertheless, the theories regarding laser and centrifuge separation do not hold up well. It is more likely that Israel's atomic bombs utilize plutonium rather than uranium for their explosive energy. Plutonium is better weapons material than uranium. Only 5 to 8 kilograms of Pu-239 are needed to achieve a critical mass, while 17 kilograms of U-235 (double or triple the amount) are required to build a nominal bomb. Finally, virtually all authorities agree that the Dimona reactor is the center of nuclear weapons research and development. This very likely is the case only because the Israelis need Dimona's most important product—plutonium—for bomb production. If its A-bombs are indeed plutonium-based, then Israel must perform separation through some method other than the LIS or centrifuge techniques.

Uranium Theft: NUMEC and Other Affairs

Complicating still further the question of whether Israel uses plutonium or uranium, and how it could separate either material, there is evidence that Israeli bombs may use both Pu-239 and enriched uranium as fissile fuel. Israel reportedly has stolen uranium, presumably for weapons purposes, on at least four occasions, most notoriously in the NUMEC affair.

NUMEC, the Nuclear Material and Equipment Corporation in Apollo, Pennsylvania, formerly headed by Zalman Shapiro, had a contract with the U.S. government to turn bomb-grade uranium into fuel for nuclear submarines. During Atomic Energy Commission inspections of 1964 and 1965, the AEC discovered that large quantities of uranium given to NUMEC for fuel conversion had never been returned to the government. Weapons-grade uranium had somehow disappeared. Subsequent investigations by U.S. intelligence agencies uncovered evidence that from 1957 to 1967 NUMEC president Shapiro had conspired with Israel to pilfer some 200 pounds of enriched uranium from his own company. (The estimated amount of missing uranium has varied, having also been placed at 382 and 572 pounds.[85])

The government's case was not strong enough to convict Shapiro, although the circumstances surrounding NUMEC's operation seemed damning. During his tenure as president, Shapiro had very intimate connections with the government of Israel and frequent meetings with its officials. The Apollo plant was often visited by Israeli representatives, including the science attaché from the Washington embassy. Weissman and Krosney write, "On one occasion, Dr. Shapiro held a meeting of American Jewish scientists at his home in Pittsburgh, at which a suspected Israeli intelligence officer asked them to get specific information for Israel. Another time he met with the same Israeli at the Pittsburgh airport."[86] NUMEC, under Shapiro, established a subsidiary nuclear company in Israel for preventing spoilage in vegetables and fruits through irradiation. The company, called ISO-RAD (Israel Isotopes and Radiation Enterprises), made Shapiro a business associate of the Israel Atomic Energy Commission. Most surprising of all, Shapiro actually employed at the Apollo plant, from which the bomb-grade uranium disappeared, an Israeli metallurgist.[87] Carl Duckett, a CIA executive at the time of the NUMEC investigation, has expressed the opinion that "the clear consensus in CIA . . . was that indeed, NUMEC material had been diverted and had been used by the Israelis in fabricating weapons."[88]

Apart from the NUMEC affair, there are other cases of alleged Israeli uranium theft. In 1968 and 1969, Israeli agents in Britain and France purportedly made daring tear-gas attacks against government trucks carrying uranium, hijacked their cargo, and smuggled the material back home.[89] According to *The New York Times*, in 1968 a ship of West German registry laden with 200 tons of uranium ore "disappeared from the high seas . . . then reappeared several weeks later under a different flag, with a different name and different crew— and without the uranium, which American investigators believed had been diverted to Israel."[90] (This theft, the "plumbat–*Scheersberg A*" incident previously described, was almost certainly planned for the purpose of obtaining uranium to feed Dimona, since "yellow cake" is best suited for fueling heavy water reactors and to help produce plutonium, not uranium, bombs.) A Central Intelligence Agency internal memorandum of 4 September 1974 states, "We believe that Israel already has produced nuclear weapons." According to the memo, this judgment was "based on Israeli acquisition of large quantities of uranium, partly by clandestine means" and on "the ambiguous nature of Israeli efforts in the field of uranium enrichment."[91] These allegations provide sufficient grounds for concluding that, in addition to plutonium bombs, the Israelis might also possess uranium weapons built from stolen nuclear material.

A-bomb Deployment

Once Israel acquired weapons-quality nuclear fuel, the designing and actual building of atomic arms would have been relatively simple. By or before the early 1970s Israel probably manufactured and separated (at its Dimona facility) bomb-grade Pu-239 (and perhaps diverted from other nations U-235 as well) and armed itself with nuclear weapons. Some CIA analysts seem to believe that Israel had several bombs as early as 1968.[92] Tahtinen, in *The Arab-Israeli Military Balance Today*, suggests that Israel had actually built "five or six" devices of 19 kiloton yield by 1969.[93] Speaking before the Senate Foreign Relations Committee on 7 July 1970, CIA director Richard Helms testified that the Israelis at that time had the means to build an A-bomb.[94] Apparently agreeing with the opinion of a *Time* special report, Harkavy writes that "the separation facility" was "completed by 1969, with the final construction and deployment of nuclear weapons accomplished between then and 1973."[95] Lefever believes that the Israelis may possess both plutonium and uranium atomic bombs, built from Pu-239 made at Dimona and enriched uranium stolen from other countries, and implies that they constructed uranium bombs before 1974. If these reports are correct, then, in Lefever's words, "Israel, not India, became the sixth nuclear weapons state."[96]

Israel's Nuclear Policy

Now that Israel is presumed to have the bomb, no one knows for certain whether it would use atomic weapons in a crisis. Nonetheless, it may be possible to determine Israel's intentions by examining Israeli actions during times of conflict and information that has been leaked by its government.

Israel's nuclear policy appears to have four main components. First, the Israelis will use the bomb as a deterrent but not as a preemptive first-strike instrument. Second, they will actually retaliate with the bomb if necessary. Third, Israel will officially deny that it has manufactured atomic arms but will imply their existence through official and unofficial channels. And last, Israel will try to prevent its enemies from acquiring nuclear weapons even if this requires military action.

Nuclear Deterrence

The thesis that Israel's nuclear policy is one of deterrence but that the bomb may be used in retaliation is most strongly supported by Israeli actions during the 1973 October War. The fact that Israel refrained from unleashing its atomic forces at the onset of hostilities testifies that the Israelis probably regard their weapons as retaliatory instruments. On the other hand, Israel's alleged preparedness to launch a nuclear counterattack when its armies seemed beaten indicates that, under extreme provocation, they are ready to exercise their atomic option.

There is another side, however, to the deterrent question. How potent a deterrent can the Israeli A-bomb be when its existence is acknowledged by Israel only ambiguously? Sporadic border shoot-outs preceding the October War must raise doubts about how truly effective nuclear muscle is in deterring international violence. The bomb certainly did not frighten terrorists into submission; their predations against Israel continued unabated after the 1967 conflict and persist even today.

The outbreak of the October fighting also brings into question whether the Israeli A-bomb is a reliable deterrent against massive Arab conventional aggression. Throughout the late 1960s and early 1970s, speculation was widespread, especially among the Arabs themselves, that Israel was building or already possessed atomic weapons.

Nonetheless, the possibility of nuclear retaliation did not deter Egypt and Syria from invading Israel in 1973. Perhaps the Arabs believed that the Israelis would not use nuclear force against them because this might provoke a Soviet counterstrike against Israel or, at minimum, would move the USSR to give the Arabs atomic weapons so that they could retaliate on their own. Russian actions during the October War, particularly their shipping of Scud missiles—allegedly nuclear-armed—to Egypt, suggest that there may have been an understanding between the Arabs and the Soviets that Russia would intervene atomically in the event that Arab armies faced total annihilation from conventional forces, or in the event that the Israelis dropped the bomb.[97] The simple fact that the 1973 October War occurred at all raises doubts about the efficacy of Israel's nuclear deterrent.

On the other hand, it is conceivable that the Arabs invaded in 1973 because they believed the Israelis had not yet developed nuclear weapons. Perhaps they felt compelled to strike quickly to overwhelm Israel before it could build atomic arms and neutralize the possibility of a conventional military solution to the "Jewish problem" in the Middle East.

Whether the Arabs attacked in 1973 because they were confident that the Soviet threat would neutralize Israel's atomic deterrent or because they believed the opposition did not yet actually possess nuclear weapons, the decision to launch the October War was evidently based on a miscalculation that nearly resulted in a nuclear catastrophe. Israel apparently was prepared to retaliate with atomic force. According to the *Time* report "How Israel Got the Bomb," alluded to earlier, at the time of the Egyptian-Syrian invasion, the Israelis already had 13 A-bombs that they could deliver via *Phantom* or *Kfir* jet aircraft. The report claims that early in the conflict, Israel's leaders, fearing that their armies were on the verge of defeat, prepared to launch an atomic counterattack. *Time* describes Israel's military crisis and its desperate decision to use nuclear weapons:

> At the start of the 1973 October War . . . the Egyptians had repulsed the first Israeli counterattacks along the Suez Canal, causing heavy casualties, and Israeli forces on the Golan Heights were retreating in the face of a massive Syrian tank assault. At 10 p.m. on Oct. 8, the Israeli Commander on the northern front, Major General Yitzhak Hoffi, told his superior: "I am not sure that we can hold out much longer." After midnight, Defense Minister Moshe Dayan solemnly warned Premier Golda Meir: "This is the end of the third temple." Mrs. Meir thereupon gave Dayan permission to activate Israel's Doomsday weapons. As each bomb was assembled, it was rushed off to waiting air

force units. Before any triggers were set, however, the battle on both fronts turned in Israel's favor.[98]

According to *Time*, the turn of military fortune, combined with a massive airlift of supplies and equipment from the United States, assured an Israeli military victory and made atomic warfare unnecessary.

Journalist Joseph Alsop believes the Israelis again threatened nuclear war against Syria and Egypt in 1974 because of a Syrian military buildup on their Golan border and the presence in Egypt of nuclear-capable Scud missiles that threatened their cities. Prime Minister Yitzhak Rabin declared that if Israel's cities were ever attacked by Scuds (in Alsop's words), "a city-for-a-city policy would be promptly adopted." Alsop interpreted this statement to be a warning that Israel was again prepared to meet Arab fire with atomic counter-fire.[99]

The incidents related by *Time* and Alsop, if authentic, suggest that Israel will rely upon the bomb as a deterrent, hoping its mere existence will dissuade attack, and that it plans to use the bomb only to respond to actual aggression and not as a first-strike instrument to preempt anticipated aggression. The alleged events further suggest that the Israelis, if attacked, are indeed willing to invoke their nuclear sanction, despite possible Soviet retaliation.

"Deliberate Ambiguity"

The *Time* report remains unconfirmed by the government of Israel or by any other official source. Nonetheless, eight years after its appearance it is still widely accepted as a true, or at least plausible, account. The Israelis might have purposely leaked this story to notify the Arabs of their possession of the bomb and their willingness to use it to protect themselves.

The Israeli government is intentionally ambiguous when it comes to discussing its atomic weapons capability. Diplomatic necessity dictates that Israel use an indirect approach, like leaks to *Time*, to inform the world of its nuclear status. If the Israelis were to admit publicly that they have atomic arms, they might alienate their Western allies, especially the United States, who are understandably sensitive about nuclear proliferation. Although Israel does not want to risk severing its military and economic lifeline to the West, at the same time it wants its adversaries to believe that it is a nuclear power in order to deter them. The Israelis have attempted to reconcile these conflicting political aims with a policy of deliberate ambiguity. They officially deny that they have the A-bomb but also officially admit they have the "capability" to rapidly deploy atomic weapons, thereby validating suspicions that those weapons already exist. Unofficially, they apparently leak reports to the press acknowledging the reality of their nuclear arsenal.

Several Middle East experts, including Jabber, believe that Israel's nuclear option strengthens its bargaining hand with the United States, enabling the Israelis to push the United States into granting most of their requests for conventional weapons.[100] In this view, the United States complies with Israel's often exorbitant demands for new conventional arms so that insecurity will not drive Israel to publicly declare itself an atomic power, an act that would embarrass the United States and further fuel the regional nuclear arms race. The possibility that the Israelis might actually invoke their atomic option in a crisis also, presumably, moves the United States to provide them with an abundance of conventional force, so that Israel will never need to resort to nuclear force. Israel's protestations that it is non-nuclear meet U.S. foreign policy requirements; its hints that it is nuclear deter the Arabs. Thus, ambiguity about the bomb best satisfies Israel's strategic needs.

The Arab Atomic Threat and Israeli Policy

Now that there is broad agreement among most defense analysts that the existence of an Israeli A-bomb has evolved from a possibility to a virtual certainty, perhaps the Arabs will be deterred from waging all-out wars against Israel in the future. Some Arab military experts admit that a nuclear-armed Israel is safer from Arab attack. Hussan Mustafa, an Iraqi colonel, once predicted that "Israel's acquisition of atomic weapons will decrease the value of ordinary weapons in the hands of Arab armies and the importance of their numerical superiority" and thereby "serve as a permanent deterrent to the Arabs."[101] Perhaps Israel's neighbors have, since 1973, refrained from invasion because they fear that the alternative to peace with Israel could be nuclear destruction.

As the only nation in the area to possess fission weapons, or at least to command the potential to deploy such instruments, Israel has, since the early 1970s, enjoyed nuclear hegemony in the Middle East. If Israel's nuclear monopoly does deter the Arab nations from waging all-out war, the measure of peace so obtained may be short-lived. Iraq, Libya, and Pakistan are believed to be working hard on their own atomic weapons. An Arab A-bomb would break Israel's atomic monopoly and could neutralize the deterrent value of Israel's weapons. Nuclear-armed bombers flying from bases in Syria and Jordan can reach any target in Israel within a few minutes and could conceivably launch a disarming surprise attack against Israel's atomic arms, destroying them so that the Israelis would be unable to retaliate for additional Arab nuclear attacks on their conventional military forces or cities. Alternatively, the Arabs could use atomic weapons to deter the Israelis from nuclear reprisal, thereby freeing themselves to resume limited or even total wars against Israel with conventional forces.

Arguing from an opposite perspective, Steven J. Rosen ("Nuclearization and Stability in the Middle East," in *Nuclear Proliferation and the Near-Nuclear Countries*) contends that if the Arabs acquire the A-bomb, the military situation for Israel might not be as bad as is commonly supposed. He suggests that a stable "balance of terror" between Arab and Israeli could emerge, with peace preserved by their common fear that another war would result in a mutually devastating nuclear exchange.[102]

The possibility of an Arab A-bomb introduces the final component of Israel's nuclear policy: maintenance of Israeli regional atomic hegemony. Israel believes that a bomb in the hands of its neighbors would pose a mortal threat and is determined to prevent the Arabs from getting one. Mossad, the Israeli secret service, has apparently sabotaged nuclear equipment stored in Europe that Western corporations had sold to Arab nations and were planning to ship to the Middle East.[103] On 7 June 1981, Prime Minister Menachem Begin made clear his country's determination to maintain its nuclear monopoly in the region when he ordered an air-strike to destroy the French-built Osirak reactor, which Begin feared the Iraqis would use to build fission weapons.[104] Mossad's sabotage activities and the Osirak incident demonstrate Israel's lack of confidence in Rosen's hopeful hypothesis that an Arab A-bomb might stabilize the Middle Eastern balance of power and contribute to peace. So far, Israel has displayed a willingness to exercise force, even to risk war, in order to preserve its local nuclear supremacy.

Other Nuclear Connections

West Germany and Iran

Nuclear partnerships with other nations continue to be an important part of Israel's atomic policy. Earlier sections have described how Israel's relationship with the United States, and especially with France, probably helped it acquire atomic weapons. But there are alleged nuclear connections with other countries as well. Some of these purported relationships have nothing more than innuendo and journalistic speculation to support their existence; others appear to have more substance and may well constitute a conspiracy on the part of Israel and its partners to develop the bomb. These additional nuclear connections, both rumored and real, deserve to be noted.

Persistent, but never proven, rumors suggest that Israel received help from West Germany in building fission arms. As early as 1957, several West German newspapers reported that Israelis and Germans were working together on A-bomb technology.[105] Zdenek Červenka and Barbara Rogers in *The Nuclear Axis* point out that in the 1950s Germany sold to Israel "the 6-MV-Tandem-van-de-Graaf accelerator, worth DM6 million, which enabled Israel to set up a department of experimental nuclear physics at the Weizmann Institute in Rehovoth." Moreover, "In 1963 the informal scientific relationship was consolidated by a joint agreement, and the Minerva Society, a subsidiary of the West German Max Planck Gesellschaft, was founded to sponsor scientific co-operation with Israel."[106] In 1965, East German president Walter Ulbricht charged that West Germany and Israel had concluded "joint preparations to produce atomic weapons" but offered no proof of his accusation.[107] The American magazine *Rolling Stone* reported, in 1977, that Israel had received enriched uranium from West Germany, in exchange for cash and scientific information, under the cover of a staged hijacking—the "plumbat–*Scheersberg A*" incident. The report alleged that Israel gave the Germans $3.7 million and some scientific secrets in payment for 200 tons of uranium ore, which Israeli commandos "By prior arrangement . . . pirated . . . from the freighter *Scheersberg A* in November 1968 as it idled on the calm seas of the Mediterranean." The authors of this article claimed they received their information from two unnamed "experts in Mideast affairs; one . . . a highly valued Pentagon consultant, the other a former National Security Agency official."[108] Israel and West Germany deny the charges.

Although the evidence for Israeli involvement in the *Scheersberg A* incident is persuasive, the accusation that there was complicity on the part of the West German government cannot be justified by the facts. The sale of a van de Graaf accelerator and joint membership in the Minerva Society do not constitute a conspiracy with Israel to secretly build atomic arms. If such criteria are used to establish the existence of an A-bomb plot, the United States should be more suspect than West Germany. After all, the U.S. contribution to Israel's nuclear capabilities—the Soreq reactor and the training of Israeli physicists at Oak Ridge and other restricted atomic centers—was far more valuable than West Germany's contribution, from both a scientific and weaponization perspective. Earlier it was established that the United States was, despite its considerable nuclear assistance, not plotting with Israel to make A-bombs. Therefore, surely West Germany, whose known aid to Israel was much more modest and far less applicable to building bombs, cannot—on this basis—be condemned of nuclear conspiracy.

Iran and Israel also were rumored to be jointly working on atomic arms in the mid-1970s, after Iran announced its plans to build two 900-megawatt reactors, with help from France.[109] But there is no concrete evidence of a conspiracy between Iran and Israel to build A-bombs. The alleged Iranian and West German nuclear connections to Israel are based almost wholly on unsubstantiated accusations and, until some proof is uncovered, should be regarded with skepticism.

South Africa and Taiwan

Egypt and Iraq have publicly accused Israel and South Africa of collaborating on the bomb. In 1978, Iraq's U.N. representative, Saadun Hamadi, denounced what he said was a cooperative arrangement between the two nations, saying, "The Zionists provide the racists with nuclear technology and receive from them uranium in exchange."[110] In this case the accusations against Israel may be correct. There is evidently some reason to believe that an actual nuclear connection exists between Israel, Taiwan, and South Africa.

The U.S. Defense Intelligence Agency (DIA) concluded, in a 1979 study, that the above relationship is real and in fact has as its aim the manufacture of nuclear weapons. The Israelis are now allegedly cooperating with Taiwan and South Africa—the "pariah nations," so-called because, like Israel, they feel increasingly threatened and diplomatically isolated—on nuclear research. Referring to the DIA study, *The New York Times* stated that "some intelligence and State Department officials who monitor the flow of nuclear technology and information are convinced that the three countries constitute the major players in an emerging club of politically isolated nations whose purpose is to help each other acquire atomic bombs. These nations have been forced to rely on each other for military and intelligence contacts as each has become progressively more estranged from the world community."[111]

Taiwan moved toward the bomb in 1976. In that year the United States discovered that the Nationalist Chinese had started operation of a small pilot reprocessing plant to separate spent uranium fuel, produced in their several nuclear reactors, into weapons-grade plutonium. Victor Cheng, secretary general of Taiwan's Atomic Energy Council, protested that the "hot cell" was for research purposes exclusively and could not be used for weapons as it could separate only a small amount of plutonium, merely 15 grams, annually. The

United States was justifiably skeptical of this explanation as it has repeatedly warned the Nationalist government not to construct such a facility. In September, the United States suspended shipments of nuclear fuel to Taiwan, whose reactors are U.S. supplied, thereby compelling them to shut down their research plant at Tsinghua University. Further pressures from Washington in the form of threatened suspension of military aid followed. In November Taipei agreed to dismantle and seal its reprocessing lab and to submit all facilities to U.S. and IAEA inspections. Lewis Dunn (*Controlling the Bomb*) says that since 1976 the Nationalists have not resumed suspicious activities in their nuclear plants. Still, their alleged research efforts with Israel in the military area, continuing after 1976, imply that, despite inspections and the closing of its reprocessing facility, Taipei has not yet given up on the nuclear weapons option. According to the 1979 DIA study, Israel and Taiwan are working together on a rocket capable of carrying atomic warheads, and today rumors persist that Taiwan, Israel, and South Africa are exchanging scientists and technology in an effort to develop long-range missiles.[112]

DIA reports that the Israelis have been cooperating with South Africa since the early 1970s and are now in that nation's nuclear power plants engaged in "energy projects" that could help the Pretoria government develop the technical expertise necessary for building atomic arms. France alleged in 1977 that South Africa then had the means and intention to make A-weapons, and the South Africans themselves have implied this. Clearly, if the Afrikaners have been working on fission explosives, Israel's involvement in their nuclear program probably is not innocent.[113] Indeed, in 1977 South Africa, perhaps with Israeli complicity, was apparently preparing to test an A-bomb in the Kalahari Desert, but was prevented by the timely intervention of the United States and Soviet Union. *Newsweek* reports "some intelligence people are convinced with . . . near certainty that" the suspected South African A-bomb "was an Israeli nuclear device. . . . Other intelligence sources believe it is possible that the Israelis only helped South Africa build a nuclear device, but they can't prove it."[114] While Israel vigorously denied any conspiracy with South Africa to build atomic weapons, according to *Newsweek*, "no senior South African official denied the reports that Israel and South Africa were cooperating to build a bomb. A query to Prime Minister John Vorster produced only a terse 'no comment.' "[115] Later, on 22 September 1979, Israel and South Africa are alleged, in a joint venture, to have actually detonated a low-yield A-bomb in the South Atlantic. But the supposed test, originally reported by a U.S. Vela spy satellite, was subsequently denied by the United States. The satellite, U.S. officials later said, mistook a meteorite for a nuclear blast test. Despite these denials, some investigators suspect that the United States is trying to cover up a real nuclear event.[116]

Whether or not the South Atlantic detonation occurred, nuclear cooperation between Israel and the "pariah" countries appears to be real. Evidently, in return for scientific assistance, Pretoria supplies uranium to Israel. South Africa has invented its own version of West Germany's "jet nozzle" technique for enriching uranium and has built a small enrichment plant.[117] The Israelis may be interested in acquiring, or may have already acquired, the "jet nozzle," which some experts believe could enable them to make uranium A-bombs. The exchange of scientific and material assistance that allegedly is occurring between Israel, Taiwan, and South Africa could accelerate Israel's mastery of certain technical skills—like rocketry and uranium enrichment—that would improve its own arsenal.

The Israeli Bomb: From Suspicion to Certainty

The conviction is widely held in the United States and other nations of the world that Israel is a nuclear military power. Despite all the evidence to the contrary others argue that the world has been railroaded into this belief by skillful propagandists. Before this chapter ends, it may be useful to demonstrate that, at least in the United States, the conclusion that the Israelis are manufacturing A-bombs formed over a long period of time, and formed fairly.

World Opinion

Over the years, world opinion regarding the development of nuclear weapons in Israel has, due to the accumulation of persuasive evidence, evolved from suspicion into virtual certainty. As early as 1957, several leading West German newspapers speculated that Israel might be working on the atomic bomb.[118] But at that time, the United States and other governments apparently rejected the West German charges. Rumors of Israeli research into atomic arms did not deter the United States from building Israel's Soreq reactor or from supplying it with enriched uranium.

The revelation in 1960 that a Negev facility, said by Premier Ben-Gurion to be a textile factory, was in fact a nuclear reactor that France and Israel were constructing secretly, greatly enhanced the credibility of accusations that Israel was working on the bomb. After the discovery of the Dimona reactor, Egyptian field marshal Abdel Hakim Amer charged, "the enemy spares no effort to obtain modern weapons with a view to securing military supremacy. . . . Israel's building of an atomic reactor in a secret way indicates Israel intends to employ the reactor for non-peaceful purposes."[119] Amer articulated for all Arab nations their conviction, vociferously and frequently expressed after the Dimona incident, that Israel was definitely planning to develop nuclear arms. The Israelis themselves reinforced Western suspicions when, in a 1963 *New York Times* interview, former prime minister Ben-Gurion hinted, in reporter C. L. Sulzberger's words, that "Israel may be experimenting with military atomics" and suggested that "weapons uses" of nuclear energy "must be explored."[120] In his book *Israel: Years of Challenge*, published in 1963, Ben-Gurion wrote, "It is not impossible for scientists in Israel to do for their own people what Einstein, Oppenheimer, and Teller—all three Jews— have done for the United States." Weissman and Krosney see this remark (which at the time was probably not missed by the intelligence community) as significant, reminding us that "J. Robert Oppenheimer was, of course, the father of the first atom bombs, while Edward Teller developed the thermonuclear, or hydrogen bomb."[121] In 1964, Prime Minister Harold Wilson called for a "nuclear-free zone" in the Middle East, thereby demonstrating that Great Britain took seriously the possibility of a nuclear Israel.[122] The United States, too, after finding out about Dimona, worried that the French and the Israelis might be collaborating on fission arms.[123] But, unlike the Arabs, the United States evidently remained unconvinced.

The United States apparently became more hopeful and assertive in its belief that Israel was not yet developing A-bombs after the Israelis, in the mid-1960s, opened Dimona to unofficial U.S. inspections. In 1965, responding to Egyptian charges that Israel would build atomic bombs by 1967 or 1968, the U.S. government replied, "neither the Israelis nor the Arabs" are "preparing to develop nuclear weapons."[124] Incautious or deliberately suggestive Israeli actions and statements further intensified Western suspicions regarding fission arms. In 1966, for unspecified reasons, Israel gave its state security prize (awarded to those who have contributed to Israel's national defense) to Ernst Bergmann, Israel's top nuclear scientist, who had served as head of Israel's nuclear development program from its inception, chairman of Israel's Atomic Energy commission, head of the IDM's military Research and Planning Division, and scientific advisor to the Defense Ministry. Understandably, the award to Bergmann fueled speculation that the Israelis were pursuing the bomb. Bergmann himself implied that this might be the case when, in a *New York Times* interview, he remarked, "It's very important to understand that by developing atomic energy for peaceful purposes, you reach the nuclear option: there are no two atomic energies."[125] In 1968, Israeli premier Levi

Eshkol said that his country had the "know-how to make atomic bombs."[126] In October of that year, *The Jerusalem Post*, an Israeli newspaper which, according to *The New York Times*, "often reflects Government thinking on foreign policy," urged Israel to develop its own nuclear deterrent.[127]

By 1968, the United States believed that Israel was working on or had already developed the A-bomb. This belief was formed as a result of several factors—the unsatisfactory Dimona inspections, the secrecy surrounding Dimona's construction and its subsequent research objectives, suspected Israeli thefts of uranium from the United States and other nations, Israel's atomic connections to France, and Israel's acknowledgment of its capability to produce fission explosives. Other evidence of an Israeli A-bomb included the discovery by U.S. intelligence that IAF *Skyhawk* jets were practicing a bombing maneuver ordinarily used only to deliver atomic weapons. In the words of a 1968 CIA report, the maneuver "would not have made sense unless it was to deliver a nuclear bomb."[128] In the same year the CIA secretly placed "sniffers" and other sensory equipment around Dimona and detected the presence of highly enriched uranium, possibly enough to make several bombs.[129] According to a previously secret report written by the CIA's deputy director for science and technology, Carl Duckett, CIA director Richard Helms informed President Lyndon Johnson in 1968 that Israel had the A-bomb, whereupon Johnson ordered Helms not to tell anyone else, not even the secretaries of state and defense.[130] Apparently fearing Soviet and Arab reactions if the United States removed all doubt about the existence of an Israeli bomb, President Johnson and subsequent administrations continued to publicly disavow any belief or knowledge that Israel had actually constructed nuclear weapons.

U.S. Middle Eastern policy, however, evidently has proceeded on the assumption that Israel either possesses fission arms or has component parts available for quick assembly. *The New York Times* reported that throughout the period 1968 to 1970, there was "some disagreement among senior government officials over whether the evidence" for an Israeli A-bomb was "absolutely conclusive. But this disagreement . . . reportedly centered at times on such narrow technicalities as the 'last-wire issue'—whether Israel should be judged to have an atomic weapon before the last wire or piece of the mechanism is hooked up."[131]

Apparently, the U.S. government's last doubts about Israel's nuclear status were eliminated later in the 1970s. In 1974, the CIA prepared a national intelligence estimate, titled "Prospects for Further Proliferation of Nuclear Weapons," expressing the agency's official conclusion that "Israel already has produced nuclear weapons."[132] On 16 March 1976, speaking at an exclusive briefing for influential private citizens, the CIA's Carl Duckett reported the agency's estimate that Israel "has ten to twenty nuclear weapons ready and available for use."[133]

Not everyone is as certain as the CIA that Israel has actually constructed fission arms. Lefever says that "despite the CIA's release of its estimates, the entire subject of Israel's nuclear weapons remains under a cloud of uncertainty."[134] In 1981, a U.N. panel investigating Israel's atomic potential concluded that it can make atomic armaments "within a very short time" but that a policy of "deliberate ambiguity" makes it impossible to determine whether Israel actually possesses bombs.[135] Nonetheless, the weight of evidence, expert opinion, and Israel's continuing refusal to sign the 1970 nuclear Non-Proliferation Treaty appear to confirm the CIA's conclusion. Today, despite Israel's "deliberate ambiguity" about its atomic status, most intelligence and defense analysts agree that Israel possesses a nuclear arsenal.

A Clever Hoax?

Israel has long argued that it has been falsely accused of building the A-bomb and is the victim of propaganda. If this is the case and the Israelis really want the world to believe they are non-nuclear, they can prove their innocence simply by opening the doors of Dimona and associated facilities to regular, unrestricted IAEA or U.S. inspections. Israel refuses to do this.

Some defense analysts have suggested that the Israelis do not possess the bomb, but rather have accomplished a fantastic deception and misled the world into thinking that they do. According to this theory, a fictional bomb would give them most of the strategic benefits of an actual nuclear deterrent without requiring them to spend any of their scarce economic and scientific resources on the manufacture of a real weapon. This hypothesis is most unlikely. The construction of the Dimona reactor and Israel's theft of nuclear materials are costly and diplomatically risky actions inconsistent with the "fictional bomb" thesis. The Israelis could fabricate a credible illusion that they possess atomic arms without undertaking these capital intensive and politically dangerous projects, which are necessary only if they actually planned to develop an atomic capability.

Israeli nuclear cooperation with France in the past, and alleged cooperation with South Africa and Taiwan in the present, is also inconsistent with the "fictional bomb" argument. Many military experts believe these associations are weapons-related. One thing Israel may be uniquely qualified to give South Africa and Taiwan is

TABLE 1.2. Chronology of Key Events, Alleged and Historical, in Israel's
Development of a Nuclear Arsenal

Year	Event
1948	Israeli geologists begin exploring Negev for uranium.
1949	Israel Defense Ministry establishes a nuclear research center at the Weizmann Institute. Work progresses on new methods to produce heavy water and to extract uranium from Negev phosphates.
1952	Israel Atomic Energy Commission set up under Israel Defense Ministry.
1953	French-Israeli nuclear collaboration begins.
1955	"Atoms for Peace," United States-Israeli nuclear collaboration begins.
	French-Israeli missile collaboration and missile tests.
1960	Soreq reactor activated.
	Israelis allegedly participate in French Sahara atomic tests.
1963	Dimona reactor activated.
1964	U.S. Atomic Energy Commission first discovers NUMEC uranium missing.
1966	Israel Atomic Energy Commission reorganized under prime minister.
1967	Plutonium separation plant (SP) purportedly under construction.
1968	Decision to complete SP allegedly made. Scheersberg A, carrying uranium ore disappears at sea. British uranium hijacked.
1969	SP reportedly begins operation. French uranium hijacked.
	First A-bombs allegedly built.
1973	Israel reportedly contemplates use of nuclear arms.
1974	Central Intelligence Agency internal memorandum says Israel has A-bombs.
1976	Central Intelligence Agency representative says publicly Israel has 10 to 20 A-bombs.
1977	South Africa allegedly attempts unsuccessfully to test Israeli A-bomb in Kalahari Desert.
1979	Joint Israeli-South African A-bomb test reported by U.S. satellites. U.S. Defense Intelligence Agency claims Israel, South Africa, and Taiwan are working together on nuclear weapons technology.
1981	"We don't have any atomic bomb now. But we . . . can do that in a short time. We . . . do have the capacity to produce nuclear weapons." - Former Israeli Defense Minister Moshe Dayan.

real, not fictional, advice on how to build A-bombs. Indeed, it is
hard to see how an Israel–South Africa "alliance" can hold together
if the exchange of nuclear weapons information is not occurring, for
if Afrikaners are really interested in peaceful atomic applications,
they would be better off making arrangements with the United States.
But if South Africa accepts U.S. help, it must permit U.S. or IAEA
inspections of atomic facilities to ensure that there is no weapons-
related work being performed. Like Israel, South Africa is unwilling
to allow inspections. These circumstances contradict the "fictional
bomb" notion and suggest that Israel must have hard nuclear weapons
expertise to sell to its partners.

Finally, it is improbable that Israel would attempt the "fictional
bomb" strategy since this policy would, in the end, defeat its own
purpose and provoke the Arabs to pose an even greater threat to
Israeli security. Whether or not Israel's A-bomb is a fantastic bluff,

the Arabs are convinced it is real and are now attempting to build their own nuclear weapons. Therefore, even if the Israeli A-bomb was originally fraudulent, the political consequence of introducing an A-bomb rumor into the Middle East—Arab pursuit of atomic arms—would compel Israel to actually develop nuclear devices itself to match the anticipated Arab threat. It is unbelievable that the Israelis, justifiably obsessed with past and possible future holocausts, would not develop atomic weapons when their enemies have declared an intention to do so.

Weak as the arguments are that Israel's nuclear weapons do not exist, any objective analysis must concede that no one, except the Israelis themselves, can be absolutely sure that Israel does in fact possess the A-bomb. Even if the Israelis were now to declare openly their nuclear status, we could not unreservedly believe them because they might have ulterior motives for doing so. Absolute certainty about the reality of Israel's atomic devices will come only when Israel demonstrates their existence to the world by exploding one of them.

Although some small residue of doubt remains about the reality of Israel's atomic arms, the weight of evidence indicates that the reality of those arms is very close to being unreservedly certain. Indeed, the existence of Israel's nuclear weapons is a virtual certainty. The evidence that the Israelis do have atomic arms is so persuasive that the United States has behaved, and must behave, in the conduct of its Middle East policy, as if the existence of Israel's nuclear arsenal is beyond doubt.

2
The Atomic Bombs

The existence of Israel's nuclear arsenal is now a "given" in the Middle Eastern strategic equation. Many articles and books have been written discussing Israeli nuclear options and how they might use their bombs to execute or threaten various kinds of atomic attacks. But there is a major deficiency in the literature on this subject: no one except Jabber, whose work is incomplete and now outdated in many important respects, has yet undertaken a comprehensive, in-depth analysis of Israel's nuclear arsenal itself to ascertain its basic characteristics. As a result of wrong assumptions about the number, power, sophistication, delivery systems, or other aspects of Israel's atomic weaponry, the numerous analyses of its strategic options and capabilities could be seriously in error. While it is true that most works on the Israeli arsenal attempt some description of its characteristics, it is equally true that most of these are cursory, shallow analyses intended to quickly dispose of a difficult task so that "more important" matters—discussing possible strategic capabilities and political consequences of the Israeli bomb—can be attended to.

An effort must be made to establish the characteristics of Israel's nuclear arsenal. There is no excuse for avoiding this task, even though facts are scarce and sources and evidence are frequently of unknown merit. Evaluations of another nation's nuclear strength almost always deal in probabilities, possibilities, and suppositions, but rarely in certainties. Since the world assumes that the Israelis have the atomic bomb, and since there is a need to assess their strategic capabilities, it is mandatory to make an educated guess about the characteristics of Israel's atomic forces, even if this means sometimes indulging in speculation and relying upon evidence of dubious credibility.

Any analysis of a nation's military strength, regardless of whether the focus is on nuclear or conventional forces, must examine the number, power, readiness, and deployment of its weapons. A less obvious, but also important, dimension of a state's strategic power is the scientific and industrial basis of its military strength. A nation's record of weapon tests, methods of manufacturing armaments, design of those arms, access to essential raw materials, and number of weapons it can make are all vital clues to a nation's technical sophistication and to its potential ability to improve the quality of its arms and increase their quantity.

Since little is known about the characteristics of Israel's nuclear forces, if the power and sophistication of the nuclear arsenal are to be approximated, an educated guess must be made about its military, scientific, and industrial features based on whatever sparse evidence is available. Israel's probable atomic testing experience, bomb-building method, bomb-design preferences, access to fissionable material, and capacity to manufacture atomic armaments, as well as the likely number, power, readiness, and location of fission weapons, are all important aspects of Israel's nuclear strength.

Atomic Testing

The question of whether or not Israel has conducted atomic explosion trials is an important one. Issues that will be discussed later in this work—for example, Israeli bomb-design preferences and miniaturization capabilities—are strongly influenced by how much testing and experimentation Israel has done. For this reason, it is appropriate to address the "test issue" at this juncture.

Israel has been accused of testing weapons or is said to have had the opportunity on three separate occasions. Lefever says, "It is possible that a bomb of French-Israeli design was tested by the French in their Sahara facility in the early 1960s . . . ," but he admits that "there is no public evidence of this."[1] The *Time* article "How Israel Got the Bomb" claims that "some Western intelligence experts believe that Israel conducted an underground nuclear test in the Negev in 1963."[2] *Time*, which does not identify its "experts," is unsupported in this assertion by any authoritative source. If any proof exists of the purported Negev explosion, it cannot be very convincing, since no government has announced it even suspects such a trial may have occurred. Finally, as discussed previously, in 1979 a U.S. Vela intelligence satellite detected a heat flash originating in the South Atlantic that, many charged, may have been a joint Israeli–South African detonation experiment. The alleged event was not recorded seismically, and further investigation found no trace of the radioactivity that should have been present after an above-ground atomic blast. The U.S. government later stated that its satellite had malfunctioned and emitted a false alarm due, perhaps, to a micrometeorite collision.[3] Although some investigators remain suspicious about this and earlier incidents, there is no persuasive evidence that Israel has ever exploded an atomic weapon.

Weissman and Krosney claim that Israel "got unrestricted access to the French nuclear explosion data," and this purportedly explains "one of the greater mysteries that has puzzled nuclear investigators for the last two decades—how Israel got the bomb but decided never to publicly test it. The Israelis did not have to" because they "had the French test results to work from."[4] Given the intimate and secretive nature of French-Israeli atomic cooperation during the 1950s and early 1960s, this theory is very believable. As already explained, however, the evidence offered by Weissman and Krosney is not conclusive, or even very convincing.

It should also be mentioned that, even if France did share with Israel its early nuclear explosion data, in the event that Israel wished to progress beyond first-generation atomic weapons, the French data would by no means liberate Israel from doing its own testing. Cooperation between Israel and France terminated before the latter was very far advanced in nuclear arms technology. Therefore, the Israelis, if they wanted more powerful warheads or smaller warheads for more flexible delivery, would have had to develop improved A-bombs on their own and perform their own detonation tests. Furthermore, even if Israel did have access to French nuclear test data, even if it was content with first-generation bombs, it would seem that the Israelis would want to independently test that data by performing their own detonation experiment just to make certain that there was no error in their interpretation and no attempt by the French to purposely mislead them. All of these arguments are, of course, merely speculative rebuttals to an unfounded hypothesis. Theories about French-Israeli collaboration on A-bomb testing should continue to be regarded as conjectural until someone can produce hard proof or authoritative testimony.

Another hypothesis contends that Israel has conducted nuclear detonation experiments clandestinely. Some argue that Israel could conduct "decoupled" underground trials in the Negev undetectable to seismographic listening and other monitoring techniques used by foreign governments to discover atomic explosions. In a decoupled nuclear test, the atomic device is placed 1,100 meters underground, suspended in a man-made subterranean cavern, and surrounded by air which, like a shock absorber, softens the impact of the blast and dampens its seismic effects. Referring to decoupling, Jabber, in *Israel and Nuclear Weapons,* states, "The larger the cavity the stronger the explosion that can pass undetected: a 10-kiloton blast would require a cavity of some 120 meters in diameter, and a 100-kiloton one of some 256 meters. . . . This technique would open the possibility of carrying out tests . . . without fear of detection."[5]

Even if it is true that decoupled tests are undetectable, the preparations required for those tests are probably impossible to conceal and would prove that a nuclear experiment was about to occur. Decoupling involves digging a shaft into the earth one kilometer deep and, at that depth, excavating a cavity wider than a football field and tall enough to contain a forty-story building and would demand a massive and highly visible commitment of men and equipment. That such a project cannot be easily, if at all, concealed was demonstrated in 1977 when reconnaissance satellites caught South Africa preparing what appeared to be an underground nuclear test site in the Kalahari Desert, an event that brought together the United States and USSR, who successfully pressured South Africa into renouncing any plans to perform a trial explosion.[6] The Middle East, troubled area that it is, is under constant surveillance by the superpowers and every other nation with an interest there. If decoupling preparations are ever undertaken by Israel, the United States, the USSR, or some other nation is certain to spot them.

Most damaging of all to Jabber's argument that the Israelis might get away with quiet atomic testing is the possibility that all decoupled blasts are now detectable. *The Washington Post* reported in 1971 that, "Such dramatic strides have been made in detecting underground atomic explosions that scientists can now discriminate between earthquakes and the smallest nuclear tests."[7] Citing the U.S. Advanced Research Projects Agency as its source, the newspaper went on to state, "The improvements in explosion detection now enable seismometers as far away as 4,000 miles to pick out weapons tests with less force than one kiloton."[8] The article claims that because of these advances, underground nuclear experimentation can no longer be kept secret.

Since the Israelis have not yet been caught performing, or preparing to perform, any decoupled detonations, and because it is doubtful that they possess the technical expertise to make decoupling preparations, it is fair to assume that Israel has not conducted any nuclear tests.

A-bomb Design Options: Uranium or Plutonium?

The United States, in the era of above-ground atomic explosions, gathered its most valuable information about the advancement of Russian, French, and Chinese atomic military science by monitoring their weapon tests. Since the Israelis do not conduct such tests, in order to gauge their nuclear sophistication we must rely on indirect means—specifically, deducing from circumstantial evidence Israel's bomb construction and design preference.

How the Israelis build fission bombs or, more to the point, whether those weapons are uranium- or plutonium-based, is the single most important indicator of their nuclear sophistication. Plutonium and uranium bombs pose different engineering problems and are associated with different nuclear engineering skills. The ability to construct bombs using only one kind of fissionable material implies a particular set of scientific skills and technical-industrial capabilities. Therefore, when we attempt to describe the scientific and industrial base of the Israeli nuclear arsenal, we are really asking two subordinate questions:

1. How might Israel manufacture uranium and plutonium atomic weapons?
2. Are Israeli A-bombs more likely to use plutonium or uranium fuel?

The Uranium Option

The first step toward constructing an atomic bomb is to acquire the explosive fuel, either uranium or plutonium. If the Israelis choose uranium, they must decide which isotope of the element they want to employ.

There are three uranium isotopes suitable for weapons use that can be obtained from commercial nuclear reactors: U-238, U-233, and U-235. Uranium-238 makes up most (99.3%) of natural uranium and so is easy to acquire. But U-238 is impossible to detonate, except in a thermonuclear device, and so cannot be used by the Israelis since they have not yet mastered fusion technology.[9] Uranium-233 is made by placing thorium-232 in a reactor and bombarding it with neutrons until it converts into U-233. Acquiring U-233 is more difficult than acquiring U-235 because it must first be made and then separated from waste materials, while small quantities of U-235 already exist in natural uranium and have only to be separated from U-238. Uranium-233 is also inferior to U-235 as bomb fuel because to produce isotope 233 one needs a neutron source of other fissile elements, like plutonium-239, that are even better suited for making bombs than U-233. (It does not make sense that a nation already possessing Pu-239 would waste that excellent, proven bomb material to make U-233, which, although theoretically capable of a fission explosion, has never been used by the nuclear powers to make weapons.[10]) Uranium-235 is the preferred A-bomb material because it is easier to detonate than U-238 and easier to acquire than U-

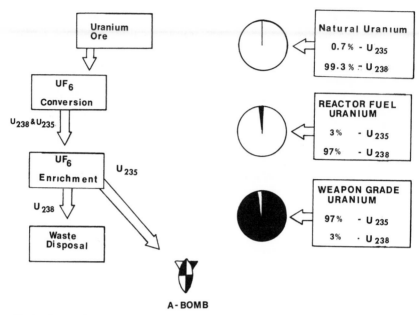

Figure 2.1   The nuclear fuel chain and uranium bomb production. The Israelis would find it difficult to obtain enough uranium to make a nuclear device. The circle at the bottom right indicates that many kilograms of U-235 with a purity of over 90% are desirable for construction of an atomic bomb. Enriching natural uranium to a concentration of even 20% U-235, the minimum purity considered necessary for practical A-bombs, is costly and technologically difficult since it requires the separation of isotopes that are chemically indistinguishable.

233. An Israeli uranium-based atomic weapon would probably employ the isotope U-235.

Nevertheless, U-235 poses its own set of problems to the bomb builder. A uranium atomic weapon should have a critical mass that is over 20%, and preferably over 90%, pure U-235.[11] (Unwieldy bombs of dubious reliability can theoretically be made from U-235 less than 20% pure, but it is doubtful that anyone but terrorists would want such cost-ineffective weapons of such limited military utility.) According to the Stockholm International Peace Institute (SIPRI), "An effective nuclear weapon based on enriched uranium would require material enriched to more than about 40 percent."[12] Separating nuclear material to achieve this purity is a difficult process, as natural uranium has only 0.7% U-235 and heavy water reactors commonly operate with fuel that is only 3% U-235 at most. Since these concentrations are too low to create an explosion, natural uranium or uranium from

Vast, sophisticated, and expensive, a gaseous diffusion plant fills a valley basin at Oak Ridge, Tennessee. The major nuclear powers use such complexes to enrich weapons-grade uranium. Israel possesses no gaseous diffusion facilities. (*Courtesy of* Science. From Robert Gillette's "Uranium Enrichment: Rumors of Israeli Progress with Lasers," *Science,* vol. 183, 22 March 1974, p. 1173. Copyright 1974 by the American Association for the Advancement of Science.)

reactor fuel rods must be enriched before it can be used in a bomb.[13] (See Figure 2.1.)

Enriching U-235 to a high level of purity is extremely difficult. Uranium-235 and uranium-238 are chemically indistinguishable, so U-235 cannot be freed from its undesirable companion element by simple chemical means. The major nuclear powers enrich uranium through gaseous diffusion. In this process, metallic natural uranium is converted into uranium hexafluoride and this hot, corrosive gas is cascaded for many months against thousands of filters, through which molecules of U-235 pass more easily than the heavier molecules of U-238. Because the weight difference between U-235 and U-238 molecules is only slight, separation of the two occurs very gradually. The gas containing these particles must be circulated through the filters about fifty times. Each circulatory cycle consists of some 4,000 separate operations that require sophisticated remote-control systems to handle the deadly gases.[14] The whole operation is extremely complex, time-consuming, and expensive.

Gaseous diffusion is too sophisticated and costly for Israel's modest scientific and financial means. Jabber explains that the power requirements alone, apart from other considerations, eliminate gaseous diffusion as a viable option for the Israelis:

> The whole operation is electrically powered and the amounts of electricity required are simply staggering. When running at full power the three American gaseous diffusion plants are calculated to consume 6,000 megawatts per year, at a cost of $205,000,000. . . . A gaseous diffusion plant tailored to Israel's needs would certainly be much smaller than the American ones (which entailed an initial investment of $2,300,000,000), but this would not render the task substantially easier, as it has been found that "the simplest possible design of a gas-diffusion plant consists of such a great number of individual high-grade components that high initial capital investments for even a minimum size installation are unavoidable."[15]

Jabber describes this enrichment method as "the most difficult and demanding industrial process there is" and correctly concludes that "gaseous diffusion is beyond the capabilities of countries even much richer than Israel."[16] If the Israelis are building uranium-based fission explosives, they must use some method other than diffusion to make highly enriched U-235.

It has been speculated that Israel might be able to enrich uranium by the gas centrifuge technique. This method of separating U-235 from U-238 is also based on the weight differences of the two elements. Gaseous natural uranium placed in a centrifuge and spun at 50,000 to 100,000 revolutions per minute will separate as centrifugal force drives the lighter uranium-235 molecules toward the outside of the whirling wheel, while heavier U-238 stays nearer the center.[17] Enrichment by gas centrifuge would be much cheaper than gaseous diffusion. J. Beckman, in "Gas Centrifuges for Cheaper Isotope Separation," suggests that centrifuges, as contrasted with diffusion plants, could reduce the cost of enriching uranium-235 by several orders of magnitude.[18] Centrifuges have been successfully utilized for non-military purposes—the Netherlands and the United Kingdom are now using them to make reactor-grade uranium (enriched to 3% U-235).[19] Jabber, writing in 1971, thought that this technology was then capable of producing much more highly enriched weapons-grade uranium.[20] Whether Israel is in fact using centrifuges to make uranium arms, however, is not known.

While there is no theoretical reason why Israel could not take the centrifuge route to the bomb, neither is there any major positive evidence that it has done so. No evidence exists, for example, that the Israelis have purchased the hundreds of centrifuges that are necessary for setting up a bomb factory. Reports, or at least rumors, of such a purchase would be expected if Israel followed the centrifuge option, since the few nations that can make this equipment—the United States and the major European powers—closely scrutinize each other's nuclear sales. Reports that Israel has had to steal enriched uranium from other countries suggest that the Israelis do not possess a uranium enrichment capability of their own. Furthermore, during the years when the Israelis are believed to have constructed their first fission arms, 1969 to 1973, the notion of making weapons-grade uranium with gas centrifuges was still largely theoretical and experimental. It is doubtful that Israel would spend its scarce resources on an untested and untried bomb-building technique when proven, surer paths to the bomb were available.

The Plutonium Option

In all likelihood, it would be easier for the Israelis to build a plutonium bomb than a uranium bomb. They can "breed" plutonium from readily available U-238 by cooking the natural uranium inside a reactor, then bombarding it with neutrons until the element converts into plutonium. This procedure does involve some risk. Technicians must be careful not to leave the Pu-239 in the reactor too long lest, under continued neutron bombardment, it degrades into Pu-240—a poor nuclear fuel subject to predetonation. Apart from this, breeding Pu-239 is not as bothersome as it sounds because nuclear reactors produce plutonium automatically, even if it is not wanted, as a natural byproduct of their operation. On the whole, making plutonium-239 should consume less time and effort than making uranium-235, and it is a superb material for bomb construction.

Once plutonium is produced in a reactor, it must be separated from impurities that have accumulated while in the reactor core before it can be made into an atomic weapon. Separating plutonium is easier than enriching uranium. Plutonium-239 is chemically different from the uranium impurities from which it must be extracted and so can be removed through several relatively simple chemical means. The hydrometallurgical method of separation involves using acid and resin beads to draw metallic plutonium out of a liquid solution. Pyrometallurgical separation achieves the same result through the use of heat. Tri N-butyl phosphate solvent extraction, the Purex process, is the most usual separation technique and involves turning plutonium peroxide or oxalate into plutonium tetrafluoride. Calcium reduces this to metallic plutonium, the basic fuel for fission explosives.[21] Chemical separation of weapons-grade plutonium is far less complex than enriching uranium through gaseous diffusion or centrifuge technologies, and it is certainly far less expensive. The three U.S. gaseous diffusion plants for uranium enrichment cost, on average, $760 million apiece to construct and over $63 million per year to maintain. In contrast India built a plutonium SP at a cost of only $7 million.[22] According to one source, "Any country with a modest chemicals industry has the capacity to purify enough plutonium to stock its atomic fuel pile."[23] Nuclear expert William Van Cleave ("Nuclear Technology and Weapons" in *Nuclear Proliferation: Phase II*) writes, "all of these" separation "processes are described in detail in the open literature and present no insurmountable problems even for the small tyro-nuclear nation."[24] A report written by D. E. Ferguson of Oak Ridge National Laboratory, and supported by other Oak Ridge atomic scientists, claims that any nation can easily make plutonium without complex reprocessing facilities. Ferguson concludes that any nation that wants to in six months can build a plant to separate plutonium from spent uranium fuel.[25] (See Figure 2.2.)

Israel is not known to possess uranium enrichment facilities, but does it have a plutonium separation plant?

The CIA believes Israel has facilities to separate plutonium, but it ventures no opinion as to their size and sophistication. Israel certainly could use its hot labs at Soreq and Dimona to serve as a small, makeshift separation plant. The opinions of Beaton and Friedman, reinforced by Ferguson, that Israel's hot labs are capable of separating Pu-239 have already been noted. *Der Spiegel*, which suggests that the Israelis are able to separate only a fraction of Dimona's plutonium, implies that their facilities are of the above sort.[26]

Proof positive of the existence of a dedicated reprocessing facility, and not simply of hot labs that might be rigged to serve the same purpose (though perhaps not so well), would officially complete Israel's technological bridge to the bomb and vanquish whatever doubts may remain about Israel's ability to separate to the highest grade all of Dimona's plutonium output. Červenka and Rogers write: "According to the data available to SIPRI, Israel's nuclear program is still at the 'research' stage; the reactor at Dimona is registered as 'research plant,' while the reprocessing plant is still assumed to operate on a small scale only. The SIPRI data is that released and carefully screened by the Israeli Atomic Energy Commission."[27]

This assertion, if true, would elevate the existence of an Israeli reprocessing facility from the realm of conjecture to an established fact, since the SIPRI data supposedly is taken directly from the IAEC itself. But Červenka and Rogers go beyond their evidence. Their source, *World Armaments and Disarmament: SIPRI Yearbook 1977*, clearly notes that it is merely assuming the existence of a reprocessing

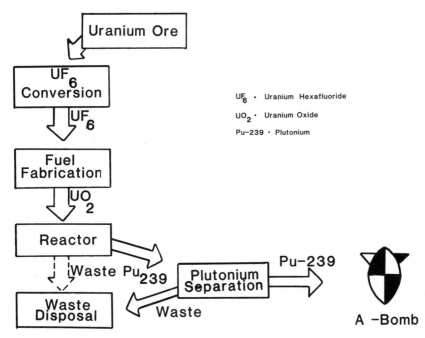

Figure 2.2   The nuclear fuel chain and plutonium bomb production. The diagram above shows the nuclear fuel chain and how the Israelis could interrupt it to produce plutonium for an atomic bomb. In the first three steps, uranium ore is chemically refined and converted into fuel. Plutonium is created as a byproduct when uranium undergoes fission in the reactor. Ordinarily, spent fuel containing plutonium is disposed of as waste (dashed arrow). But by adding a plutonium separation facility to the chain, Pu-239 can be diverted from waste disposal for use in nuclear weapons.

plant, and it makes no reference to IAEC as a source.[28] *Time,* as mentioned earlier, says the Israelis have built an SP, a term that usually refers to, and *Time* seems to suggest, the existence of a large, complex separation plant. Lefever, as already noted, writes, "large scale facilities for separating weapons-grade plutonium" exist at Dimona. The earlier testimony of former French AEC chief Francis Perrin, that when France helped Israel raise Dimona it also constructed a plutonium extraction plant, points to the existence of a sophisticated SP.[29]

Israel does have the capability to separate weapons-grade plutonium on at least a small scale in its hot labs. A more advanced SP may exist, as claimed by Červenka and Rogers and some of the testimony above, but evidence for this is more problematic.

Hot labs at the Oak Ridge Research Center. Israel has facilities like these at its Soreq and Dimona reactors for the safe handling of highly radioactive materials. Many experts believe Israel could use its hot labs for separating weapons-grade plutonium. (*Courtesy of Union Carbide.*)

The Advantages of Plutonium

According to Lefever, Israel may have "the basic materials to construct nuclear weapons by either the plutonium or enriched uranium route."[30] The possibility that the Israelis have built both plutonium and uranium weapons cannot be ignored. The Central Intelligence Agency apparently believes that Israel can construct bombs from uranium because of their clandestine acquisition of uranium and "the ambiguous nature of Israeli efforts in the field of uranium enrichment."[31] The CIA is an authoritative source, and its opinion is sufficient reason to regard Israeli uranium-based bombs built from stolen material as a serious possibility, even as probable. There are, however, insufficient grounds for concluding (and the CIA's remarks above do not claim) that Israel is able to enrich uranium for an ongoing U-235 bomb program.

It is most likely that Israel would pursue—as a continuously ongoing, self-sufficient program—the plutonium option rather than the uranium, or the uranium plus plutonium, option. The primary reason is the Dimona reactor's usefulness mainly for breeding Pu-239 for plutonium weapons and not as a source of enriched uranium-235. Research reactors and light-water reactors that consume enriched uranium are usually associated with uranium bomb construction because their fuel rods, sometimes 90% pure U-235, can be cannibalized for that purpose. However, Dimona burns natural, not enriched, uranium, and its fuel contains such low concentrations of U-235 (around 1%) that it is virtually useless for making uranium A-bombs. It is possible that the Israelis have set up a centrifuge enrichment plant for weapons-grade uranium in Dimona's hot lab, but since the reactor itself serves little useful purpose toward uranium weaponry, why would they spend millions of dollars to build the Dimona reactor? Plutonium bombs are a more likely choice for Israel if only because they justify Israel's investment in the Dimona facility. In this regard, it is perhaps significant that the Israelis themselves have compared their reactor at Dimona with India's CANDU-type (Canadian deuterium-uranium) reactor, also fueled with natural uranium, which was employed by the Indian government to manufacture plutonium A-bombs.[32]

Their hot laboratories are also evidence that the Israelis are building primarily, if not exclusively, plutonium arms. While there is some question about Israel's ability to enrich U-235, there is much less doubt that it can, in its hot labs, separate Pu-239.[33] Dimona and the hot labs constitute major visible evidence of a plutonium weapons program because the reactor and separation facilities are all that Israel needs to build plutonium-based explosives. Although a uranium weapons program is theoretically possible, evidence of its existence is less substantial and more ambiguous.

Israel is more likely to follow the plutonium path to the bomb because this avenue offers several important advantages over the uranium alternative. As mentioned earlier, separating Pu-239 is easier than obtaining weapons-grade enriched U-235. Moreover, and very importantly, where U-235 must be over 20% pure to be useful as an explosive, it may be possible to build plutonium A-bombs from much lower grades of plutonium, perhaps much less than 20% pure. Nuclear expert Robert Gillette writes, "An unclassified study by California's Lawrence Livermore Laboratory concluded" in 1976 "that even relatively simple devices using any grade of plutonium could produce 'effective, highly explosive' weapons with a yield equivalent to between 1,000 and 20,000 tons of TNT."[34] In 1977, the U.S. Energy Research and Development Administration actually built and detonated a fission weapon made from low-grade plutonium in order to prove "definitively that atomic weapons can be made from impure plutonium produced by civilian nuclear power plants."[35] The possibility that A-bombs can be made from "any grade of plutonium" should have led the Israelis to favor this material over uranium, especially if their separation facilities are not good enough to make a very pure product.[36]

Nuclear self-sufficiency is another reason for the Israelis to prefer plutonium over uranium bombs. The plutonium route to atomic arms would enable Israel to maintain a nuclear weapons industry that is self-sufficient in raw materials and that can, over a period of years, guarantee the production of enough fuel for building many bombs. Israel can import from South Africa and other countries all of the natural uranium it may need for conversion into plutonium, or it can mine uranium from its own Negev deposits. In contrast, if the Israelis cannot enrich their own uranium-235, in order to sustain an ongoing uranium bomb program they would be forced to steal enriched uranium from other nations. Theft is a risky and unreliable method of obtaining raw material, and dependence upon clandestine operations for U-235 could hinder the progress of nuclear research and development.

According to Harkavy, despite these drawbacks of the uranium bomb, "the U-235 route is preferable to the plutonium method" because "possession of significant amounts of U-235 would make it easier, at least theoretically, for the Israelis to move directly into thermonuclear weapons."[37] This opinion is at least challengeable and probably incorrect. Although H-bombs do use large amounts of uranium, especially in the bomb casing and radiation reflectors, it is not the exotic U-235 but U-238, the main constituent of natural uranium. Natural uranium is needed to develop an A-bomb whether the U-235 or Pu-239 route is taken—either track will bring the bomb builder into possession of large quantities of U-238. Furthermore, possession of plutonium may be even more important than possession of uranium-235 for developing thermonuclear arms. Plutonium-based implosion triggers can and in fact are probably preferred to ignite fusion warheads.[38] Construction of Pu-239 bombs, and especially of their complex implosion detonator systems, requires mastery of a nuclear technology that is vital and directly transferable to H-bomb development.

Finally, history suggests that the plutonium approach to the A-bomb is preferable to the uranium route. Of the world's six official atomically armed nations, five of them—the United States, the Soviet Union, Great Britain, France, and India—entered the nuclear club with plutonium devices. Only China is known to have chosen uranium over plutonium for its first fission weapon.[39]

For these reasons, if we had to attribute to Israel an ongoing program for constructing only one kind of fission bomb, the best guess would be plutonium. Nearly all of the authors cited in this book and listed in the bibliography assume that Israeli bombs are based on Pu-239. Some of them speculate that Israel might also be able to build uranium weapons, but they almost always treat this capability as subordinate to the plutonium bomb construction method.[40] Even Harkavy, who believes that "the U-235 route is preferable to the plutonium method," concedes that it probably is the case that Dimona, and so plutonium, "has been (and will remain for the foreseeable future) the only source for Israeli nuclear weapons materials."[41]

Israel may have, in fact probably has, constructed a small number of U-235 bombs from stolen uranium, but this would not constitute a continuous or ongoing program. Nor would the building of a few uranium bombs made from pilfered metal afford much opportunity for developing uranium weapons technology to a high art. Therefore, cautious evaluations of Israel's nuclear sophistication should assume that the apparatus for building A-bombs has the previously described characteristics, advantages, and disadvantages particular to the plutonium option.

A-bomb Design Options: Implosion or Gun?

Once a nation acquires plutonium or uranium, it can proceed to build nuclear arms. Bomb makers must choose from two basic designs: implosion or gun atomic weapons. The choice between these two is important because each provides technical advantages and imposes limitations upon the bomb builder that impact his ability to develop missile-deliverable warheads, higher yield A-bombs, and, ultimately, H-bombs. How do implosion and gun atomic weapons differ and what are their respective advantages in terms of facilitating further nuclear military progress? Which design is Israel more likely to use?

Design of an Implosion Device

In the implosion device, two subcritical hemispheres of Pu-239 or U-235, kept apart so they do not become a single critical mass, are placed closely together to form a spherical core of fissile fuel. At the center of the sphere, a small ball of lithium, deuterium, or tritium or a mixture of the three serves as an initiator. Surrounding the fuel core is a non-fissile sphere of U-238 that is in turn surrounded by another sphere, usually made of beryllium, and together these serve as a tamper and neutron reflector. The whole assembly is enveloped in a final sphere of chemical explosive, probably triamino trinitro benzene, that is composed of numerous individual interlocking shaped charges that collectively form a "power lens" designed to focus its blast inward.

The implosion A-bomb is triggered by detonating its chemical lens. The force of the chemical explosion drives the reflector and tamper inward, crushing the fissile fuel into a critical mass. A high-voltage neutron generator then bombards the core with neutrons, starting a chain reaction. The initiator showers the core with neutrons to boost fission efficiency. As the reaction progresses and more neutrons are freed from the fissile core, the beryllium and U-238 mirrors reflect escaping neutrons back into the core to accelerate the fission process, heating the core to several million degrees. The energy is released in an explosion of light, radiation, heat, and blast.[42] (See Figures 2.3 and 2.4.)

Design of a Gun Mechanism

The second A-bomb design, the gun type, consists of a long steel tube, very much like a cannon barrel (the original gun-configured Hiroshima bomb actually used the barrel of a five-inch artillery piece), loaded at one end with a "bullet—a subcritical mass of U-235 that can be launched down the tube—and capped at the opposite end with a larger, but still subcritical, stationary "target" mass of U-235. A neutron shield separates the two masses to prevent them from accidentally colliding and exploding. To achieve detonation, the neutron shield is withdrawn, chemical explosives fire the uranium bullet into its target to form a single body well above critical mass, and this starts a chain reaction that culminates in a fission explosion. (See Figure 2.5.)

Advantages and Disadvantages of Each Design

Both implosion and gun designs make excellent instruments of destruction, as was demonstrated when the United States used a uranium-fueled gun device to destroy Hiroshima and a plutonium implosion weapon to obliterate Nagasaki during World War II. There are, nonetheless, important differences in the sophistication and capabilities of the two designs.

The gun-type mechanism is conceptually simpler than the implosion device, which requires the minute coordination of several nearly simultaneous actions and greater knowledge of the behavior of exotic metals under high pressures and temperatures. On the other hand, the gun cannot use Pu-239 as fuel because plutonium undergoes fission much more quickly than uranium and tends to predetonate. The gun cannot assemble a critical mass of Pu-239 fast enough to maximize the amount of plutonium that will react and hence to

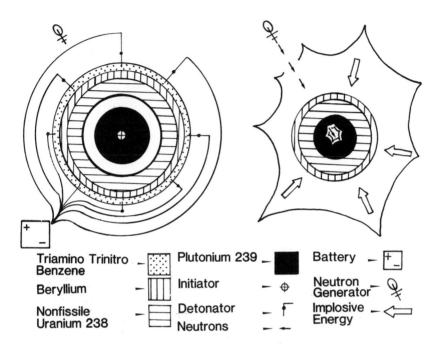

Triamino Trinitro Benzene — [⋯] Plutonium 239 — [■] Battery — [+−]

Beryllium — [‖‖‖] Initiator — ⊕ Neutron Generator — ⚡

Nonfissile Uranium 238 — [▤] Detonator — Γ Implosive Energy — ⇐

Neutrons — ←

Figure 2.3   Design and operation of the implosion A-bomb. The diagram at left depicts the main components of a plutonium-fueled fission weapon that uses the implosion method to make an atomic explosion. The implosion A-bomb consists of a number of concentric spheres. The outermost shell is a "lens" of explosives designed to focus its blast inward in order to compress the beryllium and U-238 tampers and the fissile plutonium core. An empty space between the uranium shell and the plutonium sphere allows the tampers to gather momentum before they smash into the Pu-239. An "initiator," designed to boost fission efficiency with neutron-rich lithium-6, deuteride, and tritide, is the innermost sphere.

As shown at right, the lens explodes, driving the tampers inward and crushing the plutonium sphere into a critical mass. (The tampers serve a double purpose—they ensure that compression of the plutonium occurs uniformly so it retains the spherical shape that is so important to achieving detonation, and they deflect escaping neutrons back into the fissile core to speed the chain reaction.) As the plutonium goes critical, the generator fires neutrons into the initiator, igniting it. The initiator showers the plutonium core, already undergoing fission, with more neutrons, and accelerates the fission process into an explosion.

An implosion A-bomb can detonate uranium or plutonium or combinations of both substances. Israeli nuclear weapons probably are of the implosion type.

Implosion Mechanism: 3–D Cutaway View

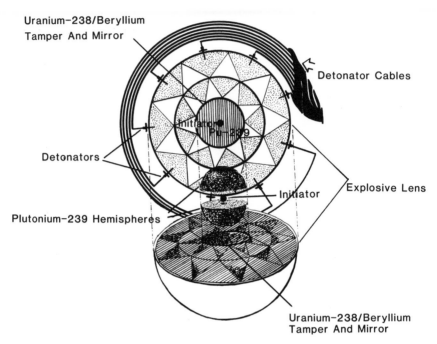

Figure 2.4   Implosion mechanism. (Adapted from a drawing by Guy Fleming in *Day of Trinity,* by Lansing Lamont, with the permission of Atheneum Publishers. Copyright © 1965 by Lansing Lamont.)

maximize the energy release of the bomb. When a gun is employed to assemble plutonium, only a small portion of the fuel undergoes fission and the reaction reaches explosive proportions too early, blowing apart the critical mass and causing the chain reaction to fizzle out before reaching its most reactive state. The implosion mechanism solves this problem by assembling the critical mass more quickly and by using the implosive force of its chemical lens to hold the mass together in order to counteract explosive predetonation tendencies, thereby allowing more Pu-239 to react and thus to release more energy. Implosion bombs can detonate either plutonium or uranium, or combinations of the two, and do so more efficiently, obtaining greater yield from their fuel mass, than gun-type bombs.

Harkavy suggests that the gun is preferable to the implosion system because the gun mechanism is easier to build and "would make it easier for the Israelis to design bombs which could be used as missile warheads (instead of requiring delivery by aircraft)."[43] While it is

FIG. 2.5

DESIGN AND OPERATION OF THE GUN-TYPE A-BOMB

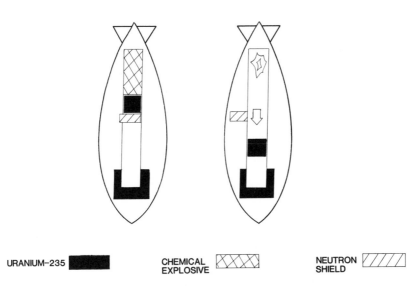

URANIUM-235 ▪▪▪   CHEMICAL ⊠⊠⊠⊠ EXPLOSIVE   NEUTRON ⧄⧄⧄ SHIELD

Figure 2.5   Design and operation of the gun-type A-bomb. The diagram at left details the main components of a uranium-fueled fission weapon that uses the gun design to make an atomic explosion. In the gun-configured A-bomb, a "bullet" of uranium-235 backed by chemical explosives rests inside a hollow tube, much like a projectile inside a cannon barrel, and is aimed at a stationary "target" mass of U-235 fixed to the tube's opposite end. A shield separates the two subcritical masses of uranium to prevent them from accidentally coming together.

As shown at right, the shield withdraws and the explosives fire the U-235 bullet into its target. Bullet and target together form a single supercritical mass of uranium that produces a fission explosion.

true that the gun is simpler conceptually than an implosion detonator, it is nonetheless no easier to construct. According to the U.S. Office of Technology Assessment, "the difficulty of actually constructing a nuclear explosive is roughly equivalent whether a gun or implosion assembly is used. The difficulties of the gun assembly are often not appreciated: a large mass of high density must be accelerated to a high speed in a short distance, putting quite unusual requirements on the gun design."[44] Harkavy also seems to overstate the latter system's superiority for missile delivery. Both mechanisms, in their primitive first-generation evolutionary stage, may be too cumbersome and heavy to be carried on rockets. (The Hiroshima gun and Nagasaki implosion bombs weighed, respectively, 9,000 and 10,000 pounds—

far too massive for even the most powerful U.S. intercontinental ballistic missile to deliver, let alone any missile available to Israel.)

Both systems, nevertheless, are adaptable to missiles. Gun A-bombs, because their design is less complex, very likely can be shrunk for rocket delivery more speedily than implosion weapons. Faster adaptability to missiles, though, does not necessarily mean that gun systems make better missile warheads. Indeed, if a choice for rocket warheads had to be made between the two mechanisms, we might infer that implosion is the preferred system, since the United States now uses an implosion trigger, not a gun device, to detonate thermonuclear missile warheads. Harkavy concedes, when it comes to missile delivery, that "the considerably higher payload weight of U-235 bombs might be an offsetting disadvantage" in favor of a plutonium-fueled implosion mechanism.[45] Harkavy is probably correct, however, that gun systems, because of their simplicity, can be miniaturized more easily than implosion systems and made into warheads for rockets in a shorter amount of time.[46] If Israeli A-bombs are gun-configured, most likely they can be modified for missiles more conveniently and quickly.

Although gun weapons would allow the Israelis to move more readily into missile delivery, implosion arms would bring them closer to developing giant A-bombs and H-bombs. A nation skilled in constructing implosion A-bombs, compared to one that builds gun-configured devices exclusively, is better equipped to develop monster fission arms, yielding hundreds of kilotons, because the design of these weapons calls for the detonation of both plutonium and uranium. Implosion systems can be modified to fission both uranium and plutonium in the same bomb, while gun systems are limited to uranium fuel alone.[47]

For the same reason, implosion technology lends itself, better than gun technology does, to the development of fusion arms. H-bombs may require the use of both plutonium and uranium.[48] Since implosion A-bombs can use both of these elements, while gun devices are restricted to one, it follows that the implosion system offers greater opportunity to work with more materials useful for H-bomb construction.

The very complexity of implosion detonation, compared to simpler gun detonation, is also an advantage when it comes to H-bomb development. Implosion and fusion systems are similarly complex in that they demand the exact coordination of tremendously destructive forces unleashed nearly simultaneously. Constructing implosion systems affords better training than building gun systems for learning how to manipulate chemical and nuclear explosions in a manner applicable to fusion technology.

Finally, since hydrogen bombs employ implosion triggers, implosion "know how," unlike gun science, is directly transferable to making a major component of fusion warheads.[49] Clearly, if the Israelis are making atomic arms of the implosion type, they are nearer than would otherwise be the case to mastering the technologies of high-yield fission and fusion.

Implosion-Configured A-bombs

If the Israelis can make both plutonium- and uranium-based armaments, their atomic bombs may be of both the implosion and gun type. This especially would be Israel's inclination if, as seems probable, it has never performed an explosion test of either kind of device. If the Israelis have not yet detonation-tested an A-bomb, they cannot be sure their nuclear weapons will actually work. Therefore, it would be in Israel's interest to construct both gun and implosion devices to protect itself from possible design failure. Since many experimental weapon variations can be made from the basic implosion and gun concepts, it is possible that no two Israeli A-bombs are built exactly alike.

Of course, the preceding speculations about Israel making both implosion and gun weapons assume that it can make both plutonium- and uranium-based bombs—a supposition that may well be true, but is by no means certain. Caution compels us to assume that Israel's nuclear weapons expertise is oriented toward, focused upon, implosion technology. Since the Israelis probably can more readily obtain Pu-239 than U-235, and since the gun mechanism cannot detonate plutonium, Israeli A-bombs are more likely to be of the implosion kind. History suggests that Israel's nuclear weapons would be of the implosion type, for all six nations that have so far exploded atomic devices utilized the implosion design in their first bombs. Even China, the only nation so far to use uranium instead of plutonium in its first A-bomb, preferred the implosion detonation method over the gun technique.[50] (See Table 2.1.)

The probability that Israel's A-bombs are all or primarily implosion-configured suggests its nuclear science faces the future developmental disadvantages and advantages that were described earlier. Specifically, the fact that their bombs are most likely implosion types is another reason to doubt that they now possess, or will soon be able to develop, miniature warheads suitable for very small missiles and artillery. Conversely, the ability to make implosion weapons means that the Israelis have cleared a major hurdle toward developing giant A-bombs

TABLE 2.1.   Characteristics of First Atomic Bombs Exploded

Country	Date of Explosion	Fuel	Design	Yield (kilotons)
United States	7/16/45	plutonium	implosion	19
Soviet Union	8/29/49	plutonium	implosion	20
Great Britain	10/03/52	plutonium	implosion	20
France	2/13/60	plutonium	implosion	60–70
China	10/17/64	uranium	implosion	10–20
India	5/18/74	plutonium	implosion	10–15

Sources: Samuel Glasstone (ed.), The Effects of Nuclear Weapons (Washington, DC: GPO for U.S. Department of Defense and U.S. Atomic Energy Commission, 1962), pp. 672, 680. "Bomb Called '45 Type," New York Times (8 November 1949). John W. Finney, "China Tests Atomic Bomb, Asks Summit Talk on Ban: Johnson Minimizes Peril," New York Times (17 October 1964), p. 1. Bernard Weinraub, "India Becomes 6th Nation to Set Off Nuclear Device," New York Times (19 May 1974), pp. 1, 8. Steven J. Rosen, "Nuclearization and Stability in the Middle East," in Nuclear Proliferation and the Near-Nuclear Countries, edited by Onkar Marwah and Ann Schulz (Cambridge, MA: Ballinger, 1975), p. 166.

and H-bombs. (Israel must still be far away from either of these weapons, however. High-yield fission and fusion arms are virtually impossible to invent without nuclear testing—*terra incognita* for Israel.)

Plutonium Production

The single most important determinant of the size and power of Israel's nuclear arsenal is its access to weapons-grade fission fuel. Since the bombs are probably all, or mainly, fueled with plutonium, the number of Israel's atomic weapons and the yield of those arms depend ultimately upon how much Pu-239 is available for building bombs.

Of Israel's two nuclear reactors—Soreq and Dimona—only the Dimona facility is available to make plutonium for military purposes. Soreq has never been usable for arms production, as it was inspected twice yearly by the USAEC from 1955 to 1965, and then by the IAEA from 1966 until today, to prevent the manufacture of nuclear weapons material. (A trilateral agreement between the United States, Israel, and the United Nations opening the Soreq reactor to IAEA inspections was signed on 15 June 1966.[51]) It may be that Soreq's hot lab serves as one of several separation facilities for Pu-239. However, the reactor cannot itself breed plutonium and almost certainly has not been tapped as a source of U-235 for uranium bombs owing to the U.N. visitations and U.S.-imposed safeguards. (Jabber claims that IAEA inspectors paid little attention to the Soreq reactor because of its small size.[52] If this is true, the facility's hot labs could conceivably have been employed to separate Dimona's plutonium after 1966. Even if the U.N. did fail to inspect Soreq, however, Israel could not secretly build bombs from the reactor's U-235, since all uranium fuel had to be returned to the United States for reprocessing.) Unlike Soreq, Dimona is completely unregulated and without safeguards, kept off-limits to international inspectors by the Israeli government, and free to make plutonium.[53] Dimona is Israel's only facility capable of breeding large amounts of Pu-239.

Estimating Dimona's Plutonium Output

How much plutonium has Israel been able to manufacture and separate since Dimona initially began operations in December 1963? The potential of a reactor to make plutonium is dependent upon the amount of uranium fuel that it fissions. According to Jabber, from every metric ton of natural uranium burned in a reactor, "some 300 to 1,000 grammes of weapons-grade plutonium can be produced."[54] He feels that a Dimona-type reactor yields 300 grams of plutonium for every ton of uranium consumed. Production of the higher figure—1,000 grams—would probably involve keeping the plutonium inside the reactor too long, in which case much of the Pu-239 would decay into Pu-240 and become less useful for A-bomb construction. A RAND corporation study, quoted in *Israel and Nuclear Weapons,* observes that "the attempt to use contaminated plutonium in a programme designed to produce reliable weapons of major military utility poses serious design and testing problems. This is particularly true for . . . less advanced nations with limited technological bases." From this, Jabber correctly reasons, "It would thus be expected of countries that are inexperienced in nuclear weapons design . . . to prefer as pure a grade of Pu-239 as they can obtain. This would hold true for Israel, particularly if she were planning to deploy her weapons without pretesting."[55] Pursuing this line of reasoning, Jabber concludes that in order to avoid the risk of contaminating their plutonium-239 with Pu-240, the Israelis probably use Dimona cautiously and breed only 300 grams of pure Pu-239 for every metric ton of uranium burned.

From the preceding observations, a formula can be derived for estimating a reactor's potential to breed weapons-grade Pu-239 based on its fission power, expressed in thermal kilowatts (KWt) or thermal megawatts (MWt). Jabber assumes that a natural uranium atomic power plant can make approximately 1 gram of Pu-239 for every

1,000 KWt days of its operation.[56] Using this equation, Dimona's total production of plutonium-239 over the last twenty years can be calculated from its known kilowattage.

The reactor at Dimona produces 26 MWt, or twenty-six 1,000-kilowatt days, and thus 26 grams of plutonium, every day.[57] Jabber thinks that the reactor is sufficiently reliable mechanically to allow it to operate at full power for 300 days per year. From this data, the facility's maximum yearly output of weapons-grade fuel can be estimated using the following equation[58]:

$$Pu_1 = \frac{MWt * D}{1000}$$

$$7.8 = \frac{26 * 300}{1000}$$

$$Pu_1 = 7.8 \text{ kilograms}$$

$$Pu_{20} = 156 \text{ kilograms}$$

Where:

MWt = megawattage (thermal) of reactor
D = days per year reactor is operating
Pu_1 = kilograms of plutonium produced in one year
Pu_{20} = kilograms of plutonium produced in 20 years

The Dimona reactor produces 7.8 kilograms of plutonium every year. This is the approximate maximum quantity of relatively uncontaminated Pu-239 that it can manufacture annually. Dimona began operations in December 1963. Therefore, as of January 1984, over the twenty years since starting up in 1963, Dimona has delivered, at most, some 156 kilograms of plutonium-239.

An alternative, more conservative, formula for estimating the Pu-239 production capacity of natural uranium reactors specifies that 0.85 to 0.9 grams of plutonium can be produced daily for every thermal megawatt of the reactor's fission power.[59] Moreover, numerous sources state that Dimona's power is 24, not 26, megawatts thermal. Using the preceding formula, and the lower power estimate, Dimona's yearly plutonium output would be 6.12 kilograms per year:

$$Pu_1 = \frac{0.85 * MWt * D}{1000}$$

$$6.12 = \frac{0.85 * 24 * 300}{1000}$$

$$Pu_1 = 6.12 \text{ kilograms}$$

This study shall assume that the prior estimate—7.8 kilograms yearly—defines the upper limit of Dimona's capacity to breed the best grade of plutonium for use in weapons.

Whatever Israel's ability to breed plutonium may be, according to a report disclosed in *Der Spiegel,* Israel is capable of separating only 6 kilograms of this bomb fuel annually. This is the only public estimate of the amount of Pu-239 that Israel can refine every year. A *Time* report says Israel's separation plant did not go into operation until 1969. Moreover, some nuclear experts, notably Lawrence Freedman, assume that Dimona's "breaking in" period lasted several years, and that it could not have begun producing substantial quantities of plutonium until the late 1960s.[60] Collectively, these various data suggest that from December 1963 to January 1984, Dimona may have produced much less than 156 kilograms of weapons-grade plutonium.

If Dimona manufactured 7.8 kilograms of plutonium every year since January 1969, it should have made, as of January 1984, some 117 kilograms of this element. From *Time*'s claim that Israel's SP went into operation in 1969 and *Der Spiegel*'s that it can refine 6 kilograms of Pu-239 annually, we can calculate that as of 1984, from Dimona's 117 kilograms of material, the Israelis have been able to separate only 90 kilograms of plutonium for weapons purposes. Alternatively, if since 1969 Dimona has bred only some 6 kilograms of Pu-239 annually, a possibility raised earlier, as of 1984 the Israelis would possess, again, only 90 kilograms of bomb fuel. Since no lower estimates of Israel's capability to produce plutonium are available (other studies assume that Israel can breed yearly more than 6 kilograms of plutonium and separate as much as Dimona can produce), this figure—90 kilograms—will be considered by this study as the minimum amount of Pu-239 available to Israel for bomb construction. The earlier number—156 kilograms—based on the assumption that Dimona has bred 7.8 kilograms of separable Pu-239 yearly since December 1963 shall delimit Israel's maximum amount of weapons-grade material manufactured. (The 156 kilograms do not include any material the Israelis may have stolen from other nations.)

It should once more be noted that the plutonium-239 production figures given here are only approximations based on the meager evidence obtainable from the public record. These figures should not be misconstrued as definitive and incontrovertible. In the absence of more reliable data, however, they deserve to be treated as a working estimate of the likely range of Israel's Pu-239 production capabilities so that the task of nuclear force evaluation can go forward.

A-bomb Design Options: Large Bombs or Small?

Israel's stockpile of plutonium-239, estimated in the preceding section at about 90 to 156 kilograms, is enough to build one large nuclear device or numerous less-powerful weapons. The Israelis almost certainly have used their plutonium to build many low-yield devices, instead of one or a few very potent "superbombs," because this option offers several significant military advantages. More numerous, but smaller, bombs can be used to assail more targets than can a lesser number of higher-yield weapons. Several small atomic devices are a more flexible deterrent than a solitary, giant "blockbuster," since they can be either hurled against an aggressor all at once, in an annihilating retaliatory strike, or committed piecemeal, one or a few at a time, to inflict limited damage upon the aggressor and to caution against further violence. A nation equipped with only one big bomb lacks this potential.

Numerous small bombs are better suited than one or a few large bombs for attacking the principal targets in the Middle East: cities, army forces deployed in the field, and oilfields. Such objectives usually sprawl over many square miles of geographic space. Several nominal weapons that, collectively, have the same yield as a solitary "super-bomb" are capable of laying waste more land space, and so are more effective in attacking these area targets. For example, although a single airburst 200-kiloton warhead can create blast overpressures ruinous to most buildings within a 34-square-mile region, the same kilotonnage distributed among ten less-powerful 20-kiloton warheads can spread the same damage over 51 square miles. Numerous small bombs are a better tactical choice than a lesser number of heavier weapons because they can destroy more enemy territory.

Last, the Israelis probably have constructed numerous low-yield bombs because high-yield bombs (over 200 kilotons) can be built only after some detonation testing, which, almost certainly, Israel has not had an opportunity to do. Consequently, they cannot be sure that any of their nuclear devices, especially big ones, will actually produce a fission explosion. (Nuclear experts generally believe Israel should be fairly confident that its atomic devices, even if untested, will work. This judgment is based on the fact that, so far, all of the nuclear-armed nations—with the possible exception of India—have successfully detonated A-bombs in their first try. India's alleged failure to produce an explosion in its first atomic test, however, is reason enough for Israel to harbor some serious doubts about the reliability of its own untested A-weapons.[61]) It is unlikely that the Israelis have invested all of their plutonium in fewer, larger weapons since this option allows them less opportunity to experiment with different designs and leaves them less recourse in the event of design failure.

On the other hand, if it is true that the Israelis did test an A-bomb in French Algeria sometime between 1960 and 1964, or in the Negev in 1963, all of their atomic weapons surely will use that one design that has been proven successful and thus will be of uniform construction. Nevertheless, even if Israel's fission arms are identically designed, the other advantages of small weapons given here are reason enough to build many modest-sized A-bombs instead of a few large devices.

In summary, then, from Israel's perspective, numbers are more important than power in a nuclear arsenal. More numerous small devices that have the same collective yield as a few more powerful weapons offer the potential to attack more targets, to destroy more enemy territory, and to experiment with more weapon designs. Therefore, Israel probably has used its plutonium sparingly in each nuclear device, building small bombs of low kilotonnage in order to maximize the number of atomic weapons that it can deploy.

How Many Weapons?

The maximum number of atomic bombs Israel can build is limited by the amount of plutonium-239 available, by its purity, and by plutonium's critical mass. (The term "critical mass" is used here to mean the minimum amount of material required to trigger a fission explosion.[62]) As explained earlier, over the last twenty years Israel could have manufactured and separated between 90 and 156 kilograms of Pu-239. The purity of this material is an important determinant of critical mass and of the number of weapons the Israelis can deploy. The greater the plutonium's impurity—the more Pu-240 and other contaminants it contains—the greater the amount of plutonium that must be used to make a single A-bomb and thus the fewer bombs Israel can build from its limited plutonium resources. For example, if the Israelis can separate their plutonium-239 to a purity of only 50% (so that every gram of Pu-239 is mixed with another gram of Pu-240 or some other contaminant), then their 90 to 156 kilograms will be sufficient to make only a very few bombs, perhaps only two or three, since several tens of kilograms are needed in each device to reach critical mass. On the other hand, if Israel's plutonium is of higher purity, less will be needed in each bomb to reach criticality, and more bombs can be built. Suppose, for example, that Israel's plutonium is very pure, say close to 100% fine; in this case, it could build weapons with relatively small quantities—less than 10 kilograms—of plutonium and so could make many bombs from 90 to 156 kilograms of fissile explosive.

Numerous sources have already been cited who assert that the Israelis possess the means to separate plutonium. As regards purity, the public record says nothing directly about Israel's plutonium separation capabilities, although there is reason to believe that Israel's plutonium is of a very pure, high grade. Van Cleave indicates that while the separation process itself is not easy, and even involves some risk, neither is it "inordinately difficult." Van Cleave:

> The toxicity of plutonium and the possibility that a critical mass might accidentally be formed constitute the main hazards of working with the substance, and require special precautions. These special precautions—shielding, remote handling, the use of glove boxes, segregation of batches, and use of processing equipment to avoid nuclear excursions—make the process a demanding one, but still do not render it inordinately difficult.[63]

One source, quoted earlier, states that according to U.S. atomic scientists, "Any country with a modest chemicals industry has the capacity to purify enough plutonium to stock its atomic fuel pile," which suggests that a nation like Israel, with a large chemicals industry, should be able to do a much better job separating plutonium than a country having a small industrial base.[64] The Ferguson report claims that the construction of a plutonium SP could be "quick and simple" and within the technical reach of almost any nation. Citing the report the *Washington Post* writes, "In the design of" Ferguson's "reprocessing plant, nothing is automated. A winery, dairy, or oil refinery could be converted to plutonium extraction."[65] If Israel built such a facility it should be able to make Pu-239 of excellent weapons quality for, according to Ferguson, the plant could separate enough plutonium to make ten A-bombs every month.

The Indian precedent indicates that Israel ought to be able to build reprocessing facilities and to separate plutonium to a very pure grade. During the 1960s India constructed on its own a plutonium reprocessing plant that was used to make India's first A-bomb. Since according to Shyam Bhatia (*India's Nuclear Bomb*), "Indian scientists estimate that six to eight kilograms of plutonium-239 are enough for conducting a nuclear explosion of ten to fifteen kilotons," India must be able to separate Pu-239 to near 100% purity.[66] Israel is India's technological equal in most respects, is technically superior in military matters, and so if India can separate plutonium to high-grade, most likely so too can Israel.

In apparent confirmation of the preceding, the United Nations and the U.S. Central Intelligence Agency both seem to assume that the Israelis can make very fine Pu-239—on the order of 100% pure—by their judgments that Israel can build a score, or nearly so, of atomic bombs.[67] Twenty nuclear devices made from 156 kilograms of plu-

TABLE 2.2. Critical Mass of Various Fission Fuels

Element	Purity (%)	Kilograms
U-233	100	6
U-235	100	17
U-235	60	50
U-235	20	850
Pu-239	100	5-8
Pu-239	12	850
Pu-240	100	6.5-10

The critical mass of uranium or plutonium, the amount of material of a given purity needed for a fission explosion, is extremely sensitive to weapon design. Taylor says the above masses "are not necessarily equal to the masses required to make a fission bomb. Using highly advanced nuclear weapons technology, practical nuclear explosives can be made with substantially smaller quantities of core materials. For some types of nuclear weapons, on the other hand, substantially greater amounts . . . are required."

Sources: Theodore B. Taylor, "Commercial Nuclear Technology and Nuclear Weapon Proliferation," in Onkar Marwah and Ann Schulz, eds., Nuclear Proliferation and the Near-Nuclear Countries (Cambridge, MA: Ballinger Publishing Company, 1975), p. 116. U.S. Office of Technology Assessment, Nuclear Proliferation and Safeguards (New York and London: Praeger Publishers, 1977), p. 143.

tonium would each use only about 8 kilograms of Pu-239, which would have to be almost 100% pure to constitute a critical mass. The U.N. and the CIA do not say directly that the Israelis can separate plutonium to nearly 100% purity, but their conclusions about the number of bombs deployable by Israel imply that they assume this capability. The U.N. and CIA estimates, the Indian experience, and expert testimony on the ease of constructing and operating reprocessing facilities all argue that the Israelis probably can make very pure plutonium.

Critical Mass

The critical mass of plutonium-239, the minimum amount that must be assembled in each weapon to achieve detonation, is another important determinant of the number of bombs Israel can build from the 90 to 156 kilograms of Pu-239 it has probably drawn from Dimona. The mass necessary to achieve a fission explosion is variously estimated at 5 to 8 kilograms of pure plutonium-239. (See Table 2.2.) Theodore Taylor ("Commercial Nuclear Technology and Nuclear

Weapon Proliferation," in *Nuclear Proliferation and the Near-Nuclear Countries*) observes that, using advanced nuclear weapons technology such as the United States and Soviet Union now possess, bombs can be made using smaller quantities of nuclear fuel.[68] It is generally agreed, however, that the capability to build A-bombs with less than 5 kilograms of Pu-239 is beyond Israel. Jabber assumes that an atomic weapon can be constructed with 5.79 kilograms of pure Pu-239, as does Arnold Kramish in *The Peaceful Atom in Foreign Policy*.[69] This study shall assume that the Israelis can separate their plutonium to a purity of nearly 100% and that 5 to 8 kilograms constitutes a critical mass.

Number of Plutonium Devices

If the low estimate of Israel's available plutonium—90 kilograms—is correct, Israel could now possess eleven to eighteen atomic weapons, depending upon whether 8 or 5 kilograms are used in each bomb to achieve critical mass. Alternatively, if the high plutonium figure—156 kilograms—is valid, the Israelis could now possess nineteen to thirty-one fission bombs, again depending upon whether each device requires 8 or 5 kilograms of material.

Testimony supporting the lower estimate of the number of Israel's atomic bombs comes from the United Nations. On 9 July 1981, a U.N. panel staffed with nuclear experts from several countries, including the United States and the Soviet Union, concluded that "Israel's Dimona reactor, which is not subject to international inspection, could have produced enough weapons-grade plutonium for ten to fifteen nuclear weapons."[70] The U.N. assessment, updated to 1984, should credit Israel with twelve to eighteen bombs. The higher estimate corresponds roughly to CIA figures, which reported ten to twenty weapons in 1976.[71] Extrapolating from the CIA's estimate, assuming a deployment rate of 0.75 to 1.5 fission devices every year since 1963, the agency assessment gives Israel between fifteen and thirty-one bombs as of 1984. (See Table 2.3.)

Number of Uranium Bombs and Extreme Estimates

The preceding figures are based on the amount of plutonium manufactured at Dimona. As discussed in Chapter 1, the Israelis may have the ability to make weapons-grade U-235 from uranium ore and also purportedly stole uranium from other countries. If the former allegation is correct, then we cannot confidently estimate the maximum size of the arsenal because the total amount of enriched uranium Israel may have manufactured over the years is unknown. Israel,

TABLE 2.3. Size of Israel's Nuclear Arsenal: Estimate of Number of
A-bombs, According to Various Sources

Source	Number of Atomic Bombs	Year of Estimate	Extrapolation: Number of Atomic Bombs, 1984
United Nations	10-15	1981	12-18
Valéry	10	1974	22
Time	13	1973	31
Central Intelligence Agency	10-20	1976	15-31

The table presents a sampling of past estimates of the number of
A-bombs. Most of these estimates were made several years ago. In the
table's last column I revise the old estimates and extrapolate an updated
figure for 1984.

In 1981, a U.N. special investigative committee concluded that Israel
had produced enough plutonium to make ten to fifteen bombs ("U.N. Panel
Surveys Israeli Atom Skill," New York Times [9 July 1981]). The U.N.
assessment may be based on the premise that the Dimona reactor did not
begin producing substantial quantities of plutonium until the late 1960s.
If, since January 1969, Dimona has made enough plutonium for one bomb every
ten to fifteen months, as of January 1984, Israel should have twelve to
eighteen weapons.

Nicholas Valéry ("Israel's Silent Gamble with the Bomb," New Scientist
[12 December 1974]) believes Dimona went critical in 1965 and thereafter
produced enough plutonium to make one A-bomb every 10 months. Valéry's
estimate would give Israel twenty-two nuclear weapons today.

Time, in "How Israel Got the Bomb" (12 April 1976, p. 39), claims positive
knowledge of the number of Israeli A-bombs in 1973: thirteen. The Time
estimate is unique because it professes to be based upon the word of
knowledgeable Israeli officials and not merely upon theoretical evaluations
of Dimona's capacity to produce plutonium. The Time article asserts that
"Israeli scientists concentrated on developing new methods for shortening
the time necessary for producing nuclear weapons" (p. 40) and built thirteen
devices between 1969 and 1973. The Dimona reactor produced only about 70
kilograms of plutonium by January 1973, so the bombs must use only 5 kilograms
of Pu-239 each or some of the weapons must be uranium-fueled. As Dimona's
cumulative Pu-239 output for the period from 1964 to 1984 is about 156
kilograms, and as Time implies that the Israelis can build bombs almost as
quickly as material becomes available, by now, given that these assumptions
are correct, Israel should have some thirty-one atomic weapons.

In 1976, the CIA announced that Israel then possessed ten to twenty
A-bombs (David Binder, "C.I.A. Says Israel Has 10-20 A-Bombs," New York
Times [16 March 1976]). If, as seems to be the case, the agency assessment
assumes the breeding of enough plutonium for about 0.75 to 1.5 (0.77 to
1.54 bombs yearly since 1963 exclusive), this gives Israel between
fifteen and thirty-one bombs as of 1984.

Many other estimates of the number of Israel's A-bombs exist, based on
different combinations of assumptions, but most fall within the range of the
figures given here.

however, probably cannot itself produce weapons-grade uranium. We can with some confidence guess the number of bombs Israel might have made from stolen uranium, as the amount of uranium obtained in their biggest, and very possibly their only, heist of weapons-grade U-235 is known. (The purported Israeli robberies in Britain and France of uranium-laden trucks, mentioned earlier, obtained "yellow cake," not weapons-grade material.) The U.S. government's Energy Research and Development Administration concluded that in the suspected NUMEC burglary, already described, enough uranium was missing to make ten bombs.[72] This estimate squares with the facts. Given that the critical mass of U-235 is about 17 kilograms, the 175.5 kilograms of lost NUMEC uranium would be enough to make ten bombs. (See Table 2.4.) If Israel did steal NUMEC uranium, and it more likely did than not, ten more weapons should be added to the size of the arsenal given here. Thus, the minimum estimated size of Israel's nuclear force would increase from eleven to twenty-one units and the maximum size from thirty-one to forty-one A-bombs. Dor-On and Teicher appear to support the latter figure (they are quoted as saying that Israel has "several dozen atomic bombs") as does Shai Feldman of the Center for Strategic Studies at Tel Aviv University, who thinks the number of devices might range from thirty to forty.[73]

The highest estimate of the number of Israel's A-bombs was made in 1981 by *Foreign Report,* a private London newsletter, which claimed that Israel has 200 nuclear devices. Another extreme evaluation comes from journalists Howard Kohn and Barbara Newman, who, in October 1977, accused Israel of stealing and illicitly purchasing enough uranium to make 150 fission warheads.[74] *Foreign Report* and Kohn and Newman do not explain the basis for their large figures, and none of the authors cited in this book's bibliography offer similarly high numbers or give any credence to these estimates.

Yet one more outlandish claim is attributed, by CBS News, to Dor-On and Teicher, who reportedly allege that in addition to making many A-bombs, the Israelis built "several hydrogen bombs."[75] *The New York Times* indicates that U.S. military experts are deeply skeptical about this and other claims by Dor-On and Teicher because neither of the authors "was in a position to gain access to nuclear information, which is the most tightly controlled in Israel."[76] The hydrogen bomb allegation casts doubt upon the credibility of the Dor-On and Teicher work because it is simply unbelievable that Israel could build fusion weapons without performing detonation tests.

TABLE 2.4. Size of Israel's Nuclear Arsenal: Minimum and Maximum Number of A-bombs Estimated as of 1984

Estimate	Total Pu-239 Produced and Separated Since December 1963 (kilograms)	Total U-235 Stolen (kilograms)	Critical Mass Pu-239 (kilograms)	Critical Mass U-235 (kilograms)	Yield (kilotons)	Subtotal A-bombs Pu-239	Subtotal A-bombs U-235	Total A-Bombs
Minimum	90	0	8 or 5		20 or 10	11 or 18		11
Maximum	156	175.5	8 or 5	17	20 or 10	19 or 31	10	41

Estimates of Israel's access to weapons-grade material, and hence of its capacity to build A-bombs, vary widely. The minimum estimate assumes that Dimona did not begin producing significant quantities of Pu-239 until the late 1960s and since 1969 has been able to separate only 6 kgs annually, for a total of 90 kgs as of 1984. This is enough for eleven to eighteen A-bombs, depending upon whether 8 kgs or 5 kgs is needed to achieve critical mass. A more liberal evaluation, the maximum estimate, assumes that Dimona has been breeding 7.8 kgs of Pu-239 annually since December 1963 and has been able to separate all of this, 156 kgs as of 1984, enough for nineteen to thirty-one weapons. Further, Israel may have stolen 175.5 kgs of U-235, making feasible ten more devices. Thus, they could possess enough plutonium and uranium to make forty-one A-bombs.

The above estimates represent low and high extremes. With very few exceptions (the exceptions are Foreign Report; Kohn and Newman, who make outlandish guesses), none of the sources cited in this work who assess Israel's nuclear strength would, judging from their estimates of previous years, place the number of Israel's A-bombs as of January 1984 as less than eleven or more than forty-one. All extrapolations from earlier realistic estimates fall in between these two extremes.

Number of A-bombs Deployed
and Production Capacity

To summarize, as of January 1984, Israel has almost certainly made between eleven and thirty-one plutonium A-bombs. Less certainly, but still probably, the Israelis are able to make both plutonium- and uranium-based arms and may have built as many as forty-one fission weapons.

Because the Israelis probably can separate 6 to 7.8 kilograms of plutonium-239 annually, depending upon which estimate of critical mass is used, they should be capable of deploying about 0.75 to 1.5 atomic bombs every year. Although estimates of Israel's A-bomb production capacity vary because of differing assumptions about its nuclear engineering sophistication and access to fissionable materials, most guesses fall within or near this range. Francis Perrin, France's former AEC head at the time of French-Israeli atomic collaboration, is "sure the Israelis have nuclear weapons. They have sufficient facilities to produce one or two bombs a year."[77] The Stockholm International Peace Research Institute offers the highest estimate of annual bomb production, claiming that the Israelis can make "several" A-bombs per year. Harkavy, on the other hand, says it is "commonly assumed" that Israel produces annually 1.2 nuclear weapons.[78]

Yield

The yield of Israel's atomic devices depends upon the amount of plutonium used in each unit and upon the skill of Israeli bomb designers. Samuel Glasstone, in *The Effects of Nuclear Weapons*, states, "The complete fission of 1 pound of uranium or plutonium releases as much energy as the explosion of 8,000 tons" [8 kilotons] "of TNT."[79] Therefore, if an A-bomb is fueled with 5 or 8 kilograms (about 11 or 18 pounds) of Pu-239 and is perfectly designed to fission all of the plutonium (a theoretical impossibility), it would have a yield of 88 or 144 kilotons. Only the superpowers and perhaps Great Britain and France, however, are probably able to fission near the theoretical maximum—about 30% of the fuel in their atomic devices— and to begin approaching Glasstone's (unreachable) ideal yield-to-weight ratio of 8 kilotons produced for each pound of plutonium used.[80] Israel, lacking nuclear test experience, is surely incapable of duplicating this achievement.

Today, Israel's bomb engineering skills, instead of rivaling U.S. abilities, probably are closer to where the United States was in the late 1940s. The U.S. Hiroshima bomb of 1945 fissioned merely 0.7 kilograms (1.5 pounds) of material out of the 60 kilograms (132 pounds) of U-235 in the bomb, to produce a yield of about 12.5 kilotons; but this was a gun device fueled with uranium. The assumption here is that all or most Israeli weapons, like the Nagasaki bomb, are of the implosion type and plutonium-based. The Nagasaki bomb was fueled with 7 kilograms of plutonium and fissioned only about 1.3 kilograms (2.86 pounds) of its available fuel. Consistent with Glasstone's observation, the bomb released 8 kilotons of explosive energy for every pound of Pu-239 fissioned, producing a yield of about 22 kilotons.[81] If Israel's A-bomb design skills are roughly equal to those of the United States circa 1945, out of 5 to 8 kilograms of plutonium in each bomb, the Israelis should also be able to fission about 15%, 0.75 to 1.3 kilograms (1.65 to 2.86 pounds), and to obtain yields in the neighborhood of 12 to 22 kilotons.

The preceding estimate of the power of Israel's A-bombs is supported by various official and unofficial intelligence reports cited in the world press and by most of the scholarly works so far published. These place the yield of Israeli weapons in the 20-kiloton range.[82] It is also significant that, to date, five of the six nations to enter the "nuclear club" did so with bombs of about 20 kilotons. (Rosen is mistaken when he claims that all of the past six entrants into the "nuclear club" did so with devices in the neighborhood of 20 kilotons yield. France is the lone exception to the 20-kiloton rule.[83] See Table 2.1.)

Van Cleave points out that, even without nuclear testing, an aspiring A-bomb nation could, by building upon knowledge and technology now widely available, initially construct weapons of surprising power for the first generation, with yields as high as 200 kilotons. France, whose first explosion measured 60 to 70 kilotons, several times more powerful than the first U.S. test at Trinity, has demonstrated the truth of this claim. Van Cleave suggests that achievement of yields in excess of 200 kilotons is not likely initially and would require several nuclear detonation tests.[84] Israel may be able to construct A-bombs having yields as high as 200 kilotons. For reasons discussed earlier, however, because in the Middle Eastern context low-yield bombs offer superior military utility compared to large ones, the Israelis probably prefer 20-kiloton weapons.

Israel's arsenal may comprise a mixed force of weapons in the yield range of 10 to 200 kilotons. But most or all of its atomic bombs almost certainly are, as previously specified, of about 10 to 20 kilotons yield, making them as powerful as the devices that obliterated Hiroshima and Nagasaki.[85]

Weapon Readiness

There is good reason to assume that Israel's nuclear weapons are not already wired and hanging from jet bomb racks but are instead hidden somewhere, dismantled. Israel's self-interest dictates that any bombs it may possess should be hidden. Keeping their atomic capability secret would allow the Israelis to declare themselves non-nuclear and to avoid alienating their U.S. and European allies, while bold parading of atomic strength might convince Israel's friends, who rightly fear nuclear proliferation, that Israel is an irresponsible "outlaw" state undeserving of Western support.

Israel's self-interest also dictates that its bombs should not only be hidden, but kept disassembled. Should definitive proof of the existence of the bombs emerge, keeping the units incomplete could import some small substance to Israel's claim that it is non-nuclear. As long as the arms are "screw ready," the Israelis can defend their non-atomic status by alluding to the neutron bomb precedent of 1978, wherein President Carter suggested that the United States did not at that time actually possess enhanced radiation weapons since those weapons were not yet deployed but were left unfinished and stored in pieces.[86] Perhaps most importantly, dismantling the devices makes them more secure against theft. Anyone who wishes to steal one of the units must first know which bomb components to appropriate and how to properly reassemble them.

Israel would gain much and give up almost nothing by storing its weapons "screw ready," according to some military experts. Martin van Crefeld of Hebrew University observes that the deterrent value of arms so maintained would diminish little. In Crefeld's words, "An A-bomb that is, or is believed to be, 'only a screw-driver away,' is nearly as effective a deterrent as one that is openly brandished."[87]

Direct evidence supporting the view that Israel is secretly storing its A-bombs in a disassembled condition comes from the previously cited *Time* Special Report, "How Israel Got the Bomb." Apparently based on testimony from highly placed Israelis, the article relates that during a military crisis at the start of the 1973 October War, Prime Minister Meir thought Israel might have to use its A-bombs and had the weapons "hastily assembled."[88] The report states that Defense Minister Dayan warned Meir of imminent defeat on the Egyptian and Syrian fronts and that "Mrs. Meir thereupon gave Dayan permission to activate Israel's Doomsday weapons. As each bomb was assembled, it was rushed off to waiting air force units. Before any triggers were set, however, the battle on both fronts turned in Israel's favor."[89]

This unconfirmed story has been widely cited and treated as a true, or at least plausible, account. In the above quotations, it is strongly implied that Israeli nuclear devices are kept partially dismantled. Elsewhere, the article suggests that Israeli engineers need about seventy-eight hours to put together and arm their atomic weapons.

It may be that Israel's stockpile of A-bombs comprises a mixture of both partially disassembled "screw-ready" and fully assembled "combat-ready" devices. The *Time* Special Report states that, after the October 1973 crisis, the bombs were sent to desert arsenals "where they remain today, still ready for use."[90] The phrase "still ready for use" could be interpreted to mean that these weapons were not again dismantled but were left complete and fully operational. In 1976, the CIA described Israeli bombs with a similar phrase "ready and available for use"—though it is unclear whether the agency's application of this wording is a signal that the bombs are "combat-ready," and not "screw-ready."[91] Perhaps the design of Israel's A-bombs is such that, once wired, the instruments cannot conveniently be taken apart again. If this is so, the weapons armed for detonation during the October War may remain activated today while those manufactured after 1973 are stored dismantled.

Here we reach an impasse. The evidence is insufficient to allow for a clear resolution of the "last-wire" issue. If forced to choose one way or the other, however, it is probably safer to say that the A-bombs are "screw-ready," since this answer more satisfactorily explains the frequent refrain of Israeli leaders, like Ephraim Katzir (former Israeli president, noted biophysicist, and former head scientist to the Defense Ministry), that Israel does not yet have the bomb but "has the potential" to build nuclear arms "within a reasonable period of time."[92] The existence of "screw-ready" A-bombs, deployable within 78 hours as *Time* suggests, would also explain the more pointed remark made in 1974 by President Katzir that Israel could acquire nuclear arms "in a short time—even a few days. If we should have need of such arms, we would have them."[93]

Weapon Storage

No source specifies the exact location of Israel's A-bombs, but it is possible to deduce where they might be from the little information that is available. The *Time* report quoted earlier states that the nuclear devices are hidden "somewhere in the desert."[94] It also mentions that they were readied "at a secret underground tunnel."[95] Confronted with a military crisis, the Israelis would very likely want to assemble their weapons on the spot, without wasting time with an unnecessary and risky trip to an assembly facility far removed from the storage site. Therefore, the bomb assembly tunnel probably is also a depot where the units are permanently stored.

The underground storage site, or sites, may be located beneath the Dimona reactor, situated somewhere nearby in the wasteland surrounding the reactor or at one of the nearby military airfields. The IAF's Hatzerim base is a notable possibility. (See Fig. 2.6.)

When the Israelis decided to build their atomic bombs, it is unlikely that they transported their Pu-239 away from the facility at all because of the possiblity of terrorist hijacking. Israel may have built bunkers for its bombs within or near the reactor that supplied their Pu-239 in order to minimize transport time and to reduce the risk of theft of nuclear material. When, on 12 June 1981, Menachem Begin accused Iraq of digging, directly beneath its Osirak reactor, a secret underground tunnel for constructing and hiding nuclear weapons, perhaps the prime minister's suspicions originated in part from his knowledge of the location of Israel's own A-bomb construction and storage facilities.[96]

Dimona's corner of the Negev is ideal for hiding atomic bombs. Situated near the geographic center of Israel, protected from Jordan by the Dead Sea and the rough country of the eastern desert, and over 250 miles distant from the nearest Syrian military bases, Dimona is one of the places least accessible to Israel's most determined adversaries. In the three wars waged between Israel and the Arab states since 1956, Dimona has largely been isolated from the fighting. Two of these conflicts have occurred since the Dimona reactor became active in 1964, and neither produced any attack, by land or air, against the facility. The isolation of Dimona, its tendency to remain a quiet backwater in the midst of Israeli-Arab cataclysms, makes it an attractive potential storage depot for the safekeeping of atomic weapons.

Another reason for suspecting that A-bombs may be hidden at the Dimona reactor is the reactor's isolation. The Negev Desert is Israel's least populous region. To suppose the worst, if a 20-kiloton atomic detonation somehow accidentally occurred here, the most destructive aspects of the explosion—blast and thermal phenomena—would little affect other settlements. The nearest neighbors, Dimona, Yeroham, Beersheba, and Arad, are far enough removed to be reasonably safe from the explosion's prompt effects. Granted, fallout from Dimona could travel hundreds of miles and threaten even the most distant Israeli city if the wind and weather conditions are right, but the danger from airborne radioactivity is by no means always catastrophic. Since the radiation hazard from fallout particles lessens dramatically

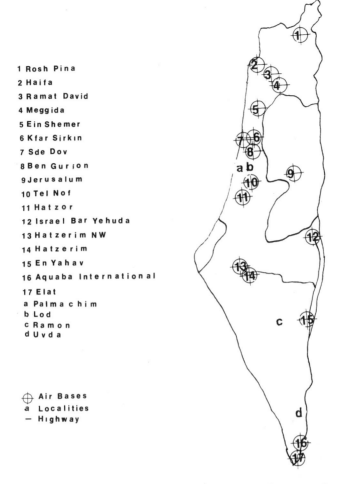

1 Rosh Pina
2 Haifa
3 Ramat David
4 Meggida
5 Ein Shemer
6 Kfar Sirkin
7 Sde Dov
8 Ben Gurion
9 Jerusalum
10 Tel Nof
11 Hatzor
12 Israel Bar Yehuda
13 Hatzerim NW
14 Hatzerim
15 En Yahav
16 Aquaba International
17 Elat
a Palmachim
b Lod
c Ramon
d Uvda

⊕ Air Bases
a Localities
— Highway

Figure 2.6   Air bases—possible nuclear launch points and storage depots. All of Israel's civilian and military air bases (shown here) are potential nuclear launch points, and every military base is additionally a potential A-bomb storage depot. The Israeli air force's ten military airfields are at Haifa, Hatzerim, Hatzor, Lod, Palmachim, Ramat David, Ramon, Tel Aviv, Tel Nof, and Uvda. (Recent tactical pilotage charts do not show the whereabouts of the air bases at Lod, Palmachim, Ramon, or Uvda, but localities bearing their names are identified above.) If nuclear weapons are stored at Dimona, a probable bomb factory, then the IAF's Hatzerim base, only 25 miles away by a good highway, is the most convenient point for nuclear launching. If weapons are not kept at Dimona itself, Hatzerim is the next most obvious choice for A-bomb storage.

(Director of Military Survey, Tactical Pilotage Chart, Series TPC, sheets G-4D, H-5A, Edition 2-GSGS [United Kingdom: Ministry of Defense, 1981]; Mark Heller, Dov Tamari, Zeev Eytan, *The Middle East Military Balance 1983* [Tel Aviv, Israel: *The Jerusalem Post* for Tel Aviv University and Jaffee Center for Strategic Studies, 1983], p. 119.)

The Dimona reactor and Negev Nuclear Research Center. The Dimona reactor underwent construction during the early 1960s. Note the large buildings near the reactor dome for accommodating labs and workshops. The complex may be where Israel's atomic bombs are manufactured and stored. (*Courtesy of David Rubinger, Time Magazine.*)

as the particles move farther from their source and dissipate through the atmosphere, by the time fallout from Dimona reaches Israel's populous northern areas, its life-threatening potential should be considerably diminished. Also, the chances are good that radioactivity originating at Dimona would not imperil other Israeli settlements but would go into Jordan or drift harmlessly over the desert. Tel Aviv, Jerusalem, and the northern and coastal cities and towns, where most of Israel's people live, would not be affected by an atomic accident at Dimona under any but the worst circumstances. For this reason, the reactor or its vicinity is a good place to store atomic arms.

Finally, the Dimona reactor's long association with the military, and its elaborate security system built and maintained by the Defense Ministry, are compelling evidence that atomic bombs are manufactured and stored there. Crosbie notes that before control of Dimona was mysteriously transferred upward to the prime minister in 1966, the facility was "under the jurisdiction of . . . HEMED, the scientific branch of the Israeli Army—which succeeded in developing a light armaments and munitions industry" and also had "the high explosives experts needed for detonating atomic bombs."[97] During the late 1960s, when Israel was probably building its first A-bombs, reportedly, no one without the highest government clearance, not even Knesset members, were allowed access to the reactor.[98]

Today, the military continues to provide security at Dimona. Army troops protect the plant, and sophisticated defensive electronic systems and radar screens operate continuously. All aircraft, including Israeli Air Force (IAF) jets, are barred from flying over the nuclear facility. This last precaution may simply be a safeguard to prevent any aircraft from crashing into the reactor and causing a dangerous radiation leak. But the Israelis are hypersensitive about Dimona. They reportedly once shot down with a ground-to-air missile one of their own Mirage 3 fighters, in June 1967 during the Six Day War, when it inadvertently flew too close to the plant.[99] On 21 February 1973, a Libyan airliner strayed from its course and the IAF downed the ship over Sinai, killing 108 of 113 passengers aboard, because Israeli officials feared terrorists might use the plane to threaten the reactor.[100]

Israel's nuclear reactor at Nahal Soreq is not as heavily protected as Dimona, nor have the Israelis ever destroyed any aircraft for violating its airspace. The reason for this may well be that Soreq is genuinely a scientific research center, while the Dimona reactor is both a factory and a warehouse for atomic bombs.

3
The Delivery Systems

Some military analysts err in suggesting that Israel can project its atomic bombs via a plethora of exotic systems. Their lists include short-range ballistic missiles (SRBMs), cruise missiles, howitzers, helicopters, and "suitcases." (Pranger and Tahtinen, for example, imply that the Israelis can deliver warheads via their Jericho MD-660 missile, the M-110 8-inch howitzer, or the M-109 155-millimeter howitzer.[1]) Some of these means of delivery are beyond Israel's present technological ability to implement; others are technically feasible for Israel, but their unreliability precludes their use.

Cruise missiles and howitzers must be eliminated as probable delivery vehicles because of one vital but often ignored fact: Israel almost certainly lacks the miniaturization technology that renders feasible the coupling of atomic explosives with very small rockets and artillery. Israel may even lack the capability to make warheads compact enough to fit on its largest missile—the Jericho—that is widely believed to be nuclear-armed. Many experts disagree with this view. Rosen, for example, argues that "small warhead construction may be . . . well within the design capacity of Israel's science and technology."[2] But neither Rosen nor any other author offers any proof of this crucial assertion, even though the entire issue of Israel's nuclear delivery capabilities hinges upon the veracity of the miniaturization claim.

Miniaturization and the
Missile/Artillery Delivery Option

Evidence and opinion are divided over the issue of Israel's miniaturization skills. Good cases can be made on both sides of the question of whether Israel can sufficiently scale-down warhead size to permit missile, specifically Jericho, delivery. The case for an Israeli miniaturization capability that would permit delivery by smaller rockets or artillery is less persuasive. This section shall examine arguments on both sides of the miniaturization issue and shall conclude that, while Israel probably can build warheads suitable for the Jericho and Lance SRBMs, its miniaturization skills are probably not so advanced as to allow for delivery by smaller vehicles.

The Case Against Israeli Miniaturization

Israel's amateur status in building and testing atomic weapons raises doubt that it yet knows how to make warheads small enough to use on missiles and in artillery. The history of U.S. nuclear weapons development implies that experience in constructing, and especially in testing, A-bombs is essential for learning how to redesign them in order to reduce their bulk and weight. The United States tested, in the "Grable" trial of 25 May 1953, the first small warhead—weighing in the neighborhood of half a ton—diminutive enough to be fired by cannons or missiles.[3] Prior to this major miniaturization breakthrough, the United States had built several hundred nuclear weapons.[4] Israeli atomic engineers, after building perhaps some eleven to forty-one bombs, are, compared to their U.S. counterparts of 1953, novices in the science of nuclear weapons design who may not yet be able to construct miniature warheads.

The decision to keep secret its nuclear status, necessitating a ban on atomic explosions, raises further questions about the advancement of Israel's miniaturization skills, for without trial detonations Israel cannot test new warhead designs. In the U.S. nuclear experience, detonation tests appear to have played a key role in progress toward making featherweight A-bombs suitable for delivery by fieldguns or small rockets. Glasstone lists all of the U.S. nuclear detonations conducted during the years 1945 to 1953, when the United States was working on many aspects of nuclear weapons technology, including miniaturization. Not all, or even most, of these tests were primarily concerned with finding ways to reduce warhead size and weight. Nonetheless, all of the explosions contributed to U.S. nuclear engineering expertise and, directly or indirectly, to its miniaturization skills. Most of these trials probably were essential to moving U.S. scientists up the learning curve until, in 1953, they finally knew enough about designing A-bombs to start making very small warheads that were cannon- and rocket-deliverable. En route to its miniaturization feat of 1953, the United States conducted at least forty-two nuclear explosion tests.[5] Before France deployed its first atomically armed missile, it performed, between 1960 and 1970, about twenty-five trial nuclear explosions.[6] As far as is known, Israel has not yet detonated even one atomic bomb. (As observed in Chapter 2, even assuming that Israel had access to French nuclear test data during the early 1960s—a dubious assumption—it does not follow that Israel knows how to construct compact warheads, since France itself had not, at the time of alleged collaboration, solved the miniaturization problem.)

Given that Israel's atomic armaments program is staffed with nuclear engineers who are unpracticed in weapons design and who do not have the benefit of explosion-test data, the widespread assumption that the small Negev Nuclear Research Center has duplicated the miniaturization achievement of the massive U.S. research and development establishment is at least challengeable. Indeed, like the first U.S. A-bombs, *Little Boy* and *Fat Man* of Hiroshima and Nagasaki, Israel's first-generation device may tip the scales at about 9,000 to 10,000 pounds.

Many experts agree with this view. Ciro E. Zoppo, in "The Nuclear Genie in the Middle East" (*New Outlook*), concurs that the Israelis lack the scientific and technological capacity to make small A-bombs.[7] Valéry concludes, "American analysts have frequently argued that several Jericho units are in service with nuclear warheads. This, however, seems to presuppose a degree of weapons miniaturization that cannot yet be justified."[8] Valéry suggests, based on the French experience, that an Israeli plutonium bomb might weigh as little as 3,500 pounds.[9] The U.S. precedent, too, could arguably support this on the grounds that *Little Boy* and *Fat Man* were hurriedly constructed and could have been made less ponderous if this had been a design objective of the Manhattan Project scientists. (Weight was not an important consideration in building the Hiroshima and Nagasaki devices because the delivery vehicle—a B-29 bomber—could carry ten tons.) But Valéry may be giving Israel's nuclear scientists too much credit, as the United States did not achieve such weight reduction until 1950, after it had performed eight detonations.[10] French bombs still weighed more than one ton as of 1965, after France had conducted eight explosion tests as part of a major effort to reduce bomb size. Moreover, the *London Times* "Insight Team" reports in *The Yom Kippur War* that military sources "close to the Israelis" say their "bombs are rather large and unwieldy and that a couple of transport aircraft have been converted to carry them."[11] The "Insight" report implies, by suggesting that few or none of Israel's bombers can easily lift its A-bomb, that Israeli fission arms are massive, indeed, and must weigh at least several tons apiece.

The Case for Israeli Miniaturization

An alternative, and stronger, case can be made that Israel has developed quite advanced miniaturization technology, even without

A

B

First-generation fission bombs. These first-generation A-bombs, built by the United States for use against Japan during World War II, may be regarded as representing the upper limit of the size and weight of Israel's atomic weapons. *Little Boy* (A), the gun-configured uranium bomb that destroyed Hiroshima, was 120 inches long, 28 inches in diameter, and weighed 9,000 pounds. *Fat Man* (B), the implosion-configured plutonium bomb that destroyed Nagasaki, was 128 inches long, 60 inches in diameter, and weighed 10,000 pounds. Israel's weapons are probably smaller, weighing as little as 1,000 to 2,000 pounds. (*Courtesy Van Nostrand Reinhold Company.* From John F. Hogerton's *The Atomic Energy Deskbook.* Copyright © 1963 by Reinhold Publishing Co.)

the benefit of nuclear explosion tests. The U.S. historical experience, wherein the development of small A-bombs required numerous trial atomic explosions, may not be relevant to Israel. The Israelis secretly could have learned much applicable to warhead miniaturization from undetectable trial detonations of high-explosive lenses (to test lens efficiency, the behavior of tampers and mirrors, and the compression of metal spheres) without performing any nuclear explosions. Equally important, critical data from the early U.S. A-bomb tests have over the years been released or inadvertently leaked and are available in the open literature. For example, detailed information relevant to designing bomb lenses, mirrors, and critical masses is available in such unclassified publications as C. L. Mader's *Detonation Properties of Condensed Explosives*, J. H. Tillotson's *Metallic Equations of State for Hypervelocity*, and H. C. Paxton's *Critical Dimensions of Systems Containing U-235, Pu-239, U-233*.[12] Israel could have bypassed the nuclear test phase experienced by the United States and proceeded directly to build miniaturized first-generation A-bombs, working with data gleaned from clandestine lens trials and from unclassified U.S. sources.

Defense expert Van Cleave believes nuclear aspirant nations, like Israel, may be capable, without testing, of manufacturing first-generation fission explosives miniaturized to only one-fifth to one-tenth the weight of the U.S. Hiroshima and Nagasaki bombs. Van Cleave writes, "An Nth country might produce initial weapons . . . weighing much less than 2000 pounds, and perhaps under 1000 pounds, without having to test them."[13] John Aristotle Philips would certainly agree with this judgment. As a junior undergraduate at Princeton University, Philips, working from the open literature, designed plans for a fission bomb that, if built, would have produced a yield of 5 kilotons and weighed only 125 pounds.[14]

Israel, it would seem, should certainly be capable of duplicating the Philips achievement, but there is no evidence it has done so. On the contrary, the "Insight" report referred to earlier indicates that Israel's weapons are as elephantine as the first U.S. A-bombs. The French experience in pursuing miniaturization, also mentioned earlier, suggests that even with access to U.S. nuclear data and with atomic testing, it may be easier to design miniaturized atomic warheads than to build them. Van Cleave implies that construction of warheads weighing much less than 1,000 pounds would require several nuclear explosion tests.[15]

The existence of the Lance and Jericho SRBMs in Israel's military inventory, having throw-weights respectively of 1,000 and 1,200 pounds, has been widely interpreted as evidence that Israel has reached the level of sophistication described by Van Cleave and is capable of miniaturizing warheads to about 1,000 pounds. These rockets are poor choices for non-nuclear military missions and their possession is difficult to justify unless they can project atomic warheads. Jericho, for example, has a price tag in excess of $100,000 dollars per rocket and is too expensive for cost-effective delivery of conventional explosives. With a CEP (Circular Error Probable—the radius of a circle within which a missile can place half of its warheads) of one kilometer, Jericho shall miss its aim half the time by 1,000 meters and so is too inaccurate to be militarily useful unless it carries an atomic payload.[16] Lance is similarly expensive and inaccurate.

It has been proposed that Jericho and Lance could be used, cost-effectively in a non-nuclear role, for suppressing SAM batteries and thereby saving even more expensive aircraft and pilots. The argument fails under close examination. There are no reported instances of SRBMs having been used successfully to neutralize SAMs. Lance and Jericho are too inaccurate to reliably destroy SAM sites that typically are hardened with revetments and shelters, and such a large number of rockets would have to be fired to disable a single battery that the attack would rapidly become, again, cost-ineffective. Nuclear delivery remains the best practical use for these missiles. The *Time* report "How Israel Got the Bomb," allegedly based on information from high-ranking Israeli officials, claims Israel can project atomic warheads via Jericho. The CIA implies that Israel has indeed so armed its rockets, as one of its reasons for thinking Israel possesses the bomb is that nation's "large investment in a costly missile system designed to accommodate nuclear warheads."[17]

On balance, the weight of evidence and argument indicates that Israel probably can miniaturize warheads to about 1,000 pounds, small enough to permit delivery by the Jericho and Lance, but not to 100 or 300 pounds, which would permit projection respectively by heavy artillery or by the Gabriel missile. Owing to the extreme ambiguity of the evidence, however, confidence in this judgment is not great. The existence in Israel's arsenal of nuclear-armed Jericho and Lance missiles is probable, but just barely. The contrary opinions of Zoppo and Valéry and the contrary evidence of the "Insight" team and of the French miniaturization experience are collectively persuasive and hard to resist. The CIA's opinion that Israel's missiles are designed for atomic warheads, and the fact that Jericho and Lance make little sense militarily without atomic warheads, are the decisive factors in my crediting Israel with nuclear armed SRBMs. There is no evidence that the Israelis possess atomic Gabriels or artillery, nor

The Gabriel Antiship Missile. (*Courtesy of* Space World Magazine.)

TABLE 3.1. Purported Israeli Nuclear Delivery Vehicles

Delivery Vehicle	Payload (pounds)
Gabriel missile	335
M-109 155-mm howitzer	95
M-110 8-inch howitzer	95

Sources: Riad Ashkar and Ahmed Khalidi, Weapons and Equipment of the Israeli Armed Forces (Beirut, Lebanon: Institute for Palestine Studies, 1971), p. 86; Robert E. Harkavy, Spectre of a Middle Eastern Holocaust: The Strategic and Diplomatic Implications of the Israeli Nuclear Weapons Program (Denver, CO: University of Denver Monograph Series in World Affairs, 1977), p. 120 fn 18; Ray Bonds, ed., The U.S. War Machine (New York: Crown, 1983), p. 101.

TABLE 3.2.   Probable Israeli Nuclear Missiles

Missile	Launcher	Numbers	Payload (pounds)	Range (miles)
Jericho (MD-620, 660)	mobile	14+[a]	1000-1500	280-300
Lance	mobile	12	1000	45[b]

[a]Jericho (CIA's name for the missile, also sometimes called the MD-620 or MD-660) is not known to be operationally deployed, and its numbers are unknown. Israel reportedly received fourteen of the rockets from France in 1970, however, and so is credited here with at least this many missiles.

[b]Lance's range has also been given as 43 to 68 miles. Robinson (below) indicates that NATO's Lance has the longer range when armed with the M234 nuclear warhead, which weighs only 465 lbs. When armed with its conventional warhead, weighing 1000 lbs., range is reduced to 45 miles.

Sources: Mark Heller, Dov Tamari, Zeev Eytan, The Middle East Military Balance 1983 (Tel Aviv, Israel: The Jerusalem Post for Tel Aviv University and Jaffee Center for Strategic Studies, 1983), p. 117.   Robert E. Harkavy, Spectre of a Middle Eastern Holocaust: The Strategic and Diplomatic Implications of the Israeli Nuclear Weapons Program (Denver, CO: University of Denver for Monograph Series in World Affairs, 1977), pp. 34-35.   Fuad Jabber, Israel and Nuclear Weapons: Present Options and Future Strategies (London: Chatto and Windus for IISS, 1971), p. 96.   Hedrick Smith, "U.S. Assumes Israelis Have A-Bomb or Its Parts," New York Times (18 July 1970), p. 8.   James E. Dornan, Jr., "Tactical Nuclear Weapons and U.S. Military Capabilities," in The US War Machine, Ray Bonds (ed.) (New York: Crown Publishers, 1983), p. 88.   Clarence A. Robinson, Jr., "Lance Delivery to Israel Expected Soon," Aviation Week & Space Technology, Vol. 102 (17 February 1975), p. 46.

is it likely that they could miniaturize warheads for these systems without performing nuclear explosion tests.

Lance and Jericho as Nuclear Delivery Vehicles

Assuming that Israel can miniaturize warheads to 1,000 pounds, an assumption that is by no means certain but nonetheless falls within the realm of the probable, then the Lance and Jericho SRBMs can be used for nuclear delivery.

Lance is a U.S. missile designed for use in Europe, where it is still deployed with NATO forces in small numbers, as a "dual capable" conventional or nuclear battlefield rocket. The missile is mounted in a mobile launcher and has a range of about 45 miles.[18] According to *The Middle East Military Balance 1983*, published by the Center for Strategic Studies at the University of Tel Aviv, Israel now has twelve of these weapons.[19]

Jericho was developed jointly by Israel and the French firm Dassault in a project begun around 1963, with the actual final production being done by the French company during the late 1960s.[20] The rocket is carried in a mobile launcher and has a range variously estimated at 280 to 300 miles. Payload is estimated at 1,000 to 1,500 pounds, but most commonly the figure 1,200 pounds is used.[21] Launchers, under the jurisdiction of the Israeli army, are apparently not visibly deployed.[22] The missiles most likely are either kept in storage or deployed in hangarettes ready for use.

The number of Jerichos available to Israel is unknown. Israel probably possesses at least fourteen Jerichos, however, as *The New York Times* reported that by 1970 Israel had received that many in one shipment from France.[23] The Israelis could well have more Jerichos than fourteen if additional, unreported, French shipments occurred or if they now manufacture the rocket themselves. This latter possibility might be the case. Shavit, an Israeli-manufactured rocket first tested on 5 July 1961, reportedly carried a payload of 600 pounds. It is not inconceivable that twenty years later Israel could be making Jerichos having double Shavit's throw-weight and greater range, especially with fully operational models from France already in hand for duplication. Plants for manufacturing Jericho engines and rocket propellants are alleged to exist near Tel Aviv. Foreign correspondent William Beecher reported in December 1971 that Israel then had, in fact, begun producing Jerichos and was building at the rate of three to six missiles per month. Based on this, Tahtinen (in 1973) calculated that Israel had at least sixty missiles (Beecher's three to six missiles monthly would give Israel some 460 to 930 Jerichos as of 1984.[24]) But if Israel ever did build Jerichos, it is probably no longer constructing the missiles, at least not at the rate cited above. Financial considerations alone, it would seem, would tend to discourage a large, sustained missile construction program. Given that Jericho is priced at over $100,000 (probably over $200,000 in 1984 dollars), manufacturing three to six rockets per month would cost $7 to $14 million annually, or about the same amount as an A-bomb project. More importantly, there have been no reports of Israeli tests of Jericho in recent years, which implies they are not building the rocket. Ballistic missile launchings (for testing reliability, modifications, and the effects of aging) are impossible to conceal from U.S. and Soviet satellites and are indispensable to any ongoing missile program.

If the Israelis can arm Lance and Jericho with atomic warheads, they will not rely primarily, if at all, upon these systems for delivery because of their very limited range. Lance, with one-seventh Jericho's range, cannot reach Cairo or Iraq. Much of Jordan and most of Syria

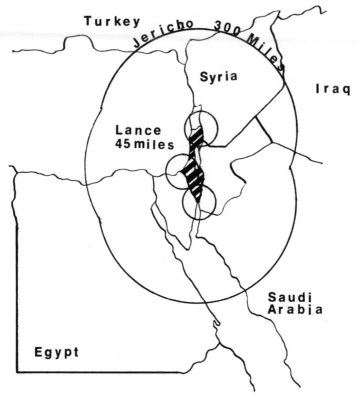

Figure 3.1   The range of Jericho and Lance.

and Egypt are beyond its striking distance. Even from forward launching positions on Israel's frontier, Jericho cannot reach the most important cities in Iraq or anything of importance in Saudi Arabia; completely outside its radius are Iran, Libya, and the USSR. With the exception of Saudi Arabia, these nations are, because of their atomic aspirations, fanaticism, or designs on the Middle East, precisely the ones against whom Israel is most likely to need a nuclear deterrent. Clearly, Israel would opt for delivery systems having longer range. (See Figure 3.1.)

Cruise Missiles

A word about Israel's alleged possession of long-range cruise missiles seems appropriate here. Dunn, in *Controlling the Bomb* (1982), briefly mentions that there is a story circulating about the existence of a

South Africa–Israel–Taiwan consortium to build cruise missiles. In 1981 the London-based newsletter *Foreign Report* asserted the existence of nuclear-armed Israeli cruise missiles able to reach Moscow. The source of the rumor is Jack Anderson's *Washington Post* column of 8 December 1980, wherein he claimed that South Africa, Israel, and Taiwan were then developing cruise missiles virtually identical to NATO's ground-launched cruise missile (GLCM). The Israeli GLCMs are mounted on trucks with multiple launch tubes (four per vehicle), have a 1,500-mile range, and are equipped with the sophisticated TERCOM (terrain contour matching) guidance system, so they can fly below radar and steer to target by computer matching of terrain contours. Apart from alluding to anonymous U.S. government officials, Anderson does not identify his sources.[25]

The cruise missile story is certainly not based on any understanding of what is technically possible, and technically impossible, for Israel. The U.S. Tomahawk BGM-109G cruise missiles, the type Anderson seems to have in mind, carry payloads in the low hundreds of pounds and so could not deliver Israeli warheads that weigh at least, and very possibly more than, 1,000 pounds. More importantly, the combined resources of a South Africa–Israel–Taiwan union could not develop TERCOM, the product of the most advanced U.S. computer and software technology—even now not fully perfected. Israel and its supposed partners, possessing only modest semiconductor and software industries, simply lack the technological base to attempt development of a TERCOM-guided GLCM. The cruise missile rumor may safely be dismissed as nonsense.

Improbable Delivery Vehicles:
Transport Aircraft, Helicopters, and "Suitcases"

Harkavy suggests that the Israelis could deliver nuclear arms to target via civil or military transport, helicopter, or "suitcase,"[26] while acknowledging that the actual use of any of these vehicles is highly unlikely.

Transport planes—like El Al passenger Boeings or C-130 supply ships—do offer some advantages over military fighter-bombers. They can lift heavier payloads (and so could more easily carry a first-generation nuclear weapon weighing many thousands of pounds) and can fly farther than most military attack aircraft. Their main disadvantage is their vulnerability. Slow-flying transports can be destroyed by surface-to-air missiles (SAMs) or interceptors practically at will. An El Al ship or a C-130 would presumably rely upon its nonthreatening appearance to get through enemy air defenses. Even in the midst of a war, it is conceivable that a transport carrying a warhead, but claiming to be loaded with civilian passengers and to be off-course or in need of making an emergency landing, might be allowed to fly unmolested over hostile territory, or even to land at an enemy city. Of course, any delivery method that relies for success upon the good will of the enemy is not likely to be used by Israel. The Israelis themselves demonstrated the impracticality of using transports as nuclear delivery vehicles shortly after the October War when they shot down a Libyan airliner, loaded with civilians, which had wandered into their airspace.[27]

Helicopters would be no better than transport aircraft for executing nuclear missions. These machines have an advantage over transports in that they can skim low over the ground and cruise below enemy radar to effect delivery, but they are poor atomic couriers. Ordinarily, they cannot fly high enough to get out of range of antiaircraft (AA) guns and are easy prey for SAMs and interceptors. Flying at low altitude, as they would on a nuclear strike to elude radar, helicopters are vulnerable to infantry small-arms fire. If the enemy felled a roof-skimming, A-bomb-laden chopper, the helicopter's low-altitude crash might not wreck its nuclear cargo and the enemy could possibly capture its weapon intact. The IAF undoubtedly takes a dim view of a delivery system that might give an Israeli bomb to terrorists.

Delivery by "suitcase"—that is, clandestinely assembling a warhead near the target—is also remotely possible. Shipping conventional explosives via car or truck, to be detonated in an enemy city, is not uncommon in the Middle East, and this variation on "suitcase" tactics also could be employed with nuclear explosives. Chauffeuring an A-bomb to target might be the only way to strike an opponent like the Soviet Union, whose dense air defenses might prohibit penetration by Israeli jets. If bombers cannot pierce the Soviet air screen, perhaps a commercial truck could smuggle an A-bomb across the USSR's border and reach a major city. (Former prime minister Begin, in his guerrilla days, once successfully used trucks to send large conventional bombs to his enemies.[28] It is not impossible that another prime minister might, in an ultimate crisis, return to this old-fashioned delivery method to hit an otherwise unreachable enemy city, like Moscow.) Even though carrying A-bombs to target "suitcase"-style might make sense under rare circumstances, in most nuclear scenarios, it would not be a serious alternative. "Suitcase" delivery is so clearly fraught with risk and uncertainty that projection via El Al Boeing or helicopter is preferable.

Probable Delivery Vehicles: Nuclear Bombers

Since Israel's missiles have very limited range, and because other means of projection are too unreliable, it is probable that the Israelis would rely primarily, if not exclusively, on jet aircraft to carry their atomic weapons. In addition to superior reach, the latest aircraft (like F-15 and F-16) offer much better accuracy than the missiles. From among the many fighter-bombers available to the IAF, Israel's most likely choice of jet for a nuclear mission can be narrowed to a few specific aircraft.

Six different jets constitute the main-line strength of the IAF: the F-15 Eagle, F-16 Fighting Falcon, F-4 Phantom, Kfir, Skyhawk A-4, and Mirage 3CJ.[29] Assuming that a first-generation Israeli bomb weighs about 1,000 pounds, though all of the planes can be used for delivery, Mirage 3CJ can be excluded at the outset as a front-ranked choice for a nuclear bomber. Because the ratio of Mirage's payload capacity to bomb weight is markedly inferior compared to the other aircraft, a 1,000-pound weapon might more seriously reduce its speed and maneuverability, render the plane more vulnerable to SAMs and interceptors, and so decrease its chances of reaching target. Valéry says of the Mirage 3CJ, "It is certainly difficult to imagine it as a strategic bomber." He points out that "the French . . . had to beef up their Mirage 3 . . . to make it into the Mirage 4 nuclear bomber. Two engines had to be used and the wing area doubled in the process."[30] If instead of weighing 1,000 pounds Israeli A-bombs weigh 9,000 to 10,000 pounds apiece, a closely competing lesser possibility, then Mirage 3CJ cannot serve as a delivery system at all because its maximum lift capacity—3,000 pounds—is inadequate to handle such a massive device.

Two other aircraft, Kfir and Skyhawk A-4, with respective weight limits of 9,468 and 9,155 pounds can easily handle a 1,000-pound A-bomb, but are only marginally suited for carrying a 9,000- to 10,000-pound weapon.

Assuming that Israel's bomb weighs 1,000 and not 10,000 pounds, five of the six jets noted in Table 3.3, excluding Mirage 3CJ, are front-line selections for performing nuclear delivery. From among these candidates, the choices can be still further reduced by measuring

TABLE 3.3. Potential Israeli Nuclear Bombers: A Comparison of Payload and Range Characteristics

Aircraft	Numbers	Payload (pounds)	Minimum Range (miles)	Maximum Range (miles)
F-16 Falcon	75	12,000	575	1150
F-15 Eagle	40	16,000	1209	2419
F-4 Phantom	160	16,000	712	1424
Kfir	180	9,468	477	954
A-4 Skyhawk	185	9,155	335	670
Mirage 3CJ	30	3,000	560	1120

Payload refers to the total weight that an aircraft can carry on all of its pylons and hardpoints. Minimum range figures assume each jet is lifting maximum payload (an A-bomb weighing 1,000 to 9,000 pounds plus whatever defensive armament can be added) and making a round-trip--from base to target and back to base again. Maximum range figures assume each jet is lifting maximum payload and making a one-way trip--from base to the farthest possible distance. Now under development is a new fighter-bomber, the Iai Lavi ("Young Lion"), that is expected to have a payload of 6,000 pounds and a combat radius of 281 miles when fully loaded. It will replace Skyhawk when deployed in the 1990s.

Sources: John W. R. Taylor, ed., Jane's All the World's Aircraft 1982-1983 (London: Jane's Publishing Co., 1982), pp. 122-123, 369-374, 415-416; Jane's . . . 1980-1981 (1980), pp. 111, 346-347, 381-383; Jane's . . . 1968-1969 (1968), p. 39; Bill Gunston, An Illustrated Guide to Modern Fighters and Attack Aircraft (New York: Arco, 1980); Steven L. Rys, U.S. Military Power (Greenwich, CT: Bison Books, 1983), p. 121; Tom Gervasi, Arsenal of Democracy (New York: Grove Press, 1981), p. 118; Mark Heller, Dov Tamari, and Zeev Eytan, The Middle East Military Balance 1983 (Tel Aviv: The Jerusalem Post for Tel Aviv University and Jaffee Center for Strategic Studies, 1983), p. 118.

each plane's performance against two salient criteria: penetration and range capabilities.

Nuclear Bomber Candidates: Penetration Capabilities Compared

The IAF will require its bomber to offer the best penetration characteristics to ensure the successful breaching of enemy air defenses and delivery of the atomic payload. The ability of a bomber to pierce air defenses depends largely upon its electronic warfare (EW) avionics and combat qualities. EW systems determine whether (and how well) a bomber can fly below enemy radar, identify and evade possible SAM and interceptor threats, jam enemy electronic countermeasures, and perform other such tasks essential to air defense penetration. If all else fails, a bomber's combat characteristics—its maneuverability, avionics, armaments, and speed—will decide whether the aircraft can fight its way through enemy defenses and complete its mission.

The F-15 Eagle and the F-16 Falcon are armed with modified versions of the most advanced U.S. electronic warfare equipment. Avionics superiority over other planes gives them a considerable advantage in air defense penetration. Pulse-Doppler radar enables F-15 to track other aircraft at long range, down to treetop level, while its new interrogator can tell whether the spotted plane is friend or foe. Conversely, Eagle's radar warning system notifies the pilot when his jet is being tracked so that he can activate an electronic countermeasure unit and jam the enemy radar signals.

F-15's new air data computer and inertial guidance system allow the pilot to fly virtually blind at all altitudes and in all weather conditions, rely almost entirely on cathode ray tube (CRT) readouts for guidance and steering instructions, and navigate unerringly to target. Using the same systems, Eagle can fix its global coordinates and, given enough fuel, steer its way to any point on earth.[31] These navigational capabilities would prove invaluable to a bomber that must fly at low altitudes during inclement weather or on long missions over hundreds of miles of territory unfamiliar to the pilot. Eagle is also equipped with a heads-up display targeting system, very useful for dogfights, that presents the pilot with an eye-level picture of all data needed to intercept and destroy an enemy aircraft, without requiring the pilot to glance away from his target. F-15 can track up to twenty enemy jets simultaneously. Some F-16 avionics are made by different companies in dissimilar configurations, but they are equally advanced and offer most of the same capabilities as those on F-15. Even though the EW systems of F-15 and F-16 are "degraded" by the United States before being exported to Israel, these jets nonetheless remain electronically superior to their rivals.[32] Other aircraft can do many of the same things as Falcon and Eagle—detecting and jamming radar, for example—but their avionics are older, not as advanced technically, and cannot do the job as well. F-15 has the additional advantage of being one of the world's highest altitude combat aircraft. Eagle has a ceiling of 65,000 feet, compared to 55,000 to 60,000 feet for Mig-21 or Mig-23, and so can overfly by one or two miles most interceptors available to the Arabs.

The superiority of Falcon and Eagle over all other fighters in avionics, speed, maneuverability, and other combat qualities is well known. F-15 and F-16, the newest and most advanced U.S. military aircraft, are air superiority weapons—designed to individually combat several enemy aircraft simultaneously—and are generally conceded to be the best fighters in the world. Should necessity so demand, these planes are better able than any others to battle their way through enemy defenses in order to reach target.

The penetration capabilities of Eagle and Falcon were demonstrated on 7 June 1981, during "Operation Babylon," when Israel sent these planes to destroy Iraq's Osirak reactor, located near Baghdad. (As mentioned earlier, Premier Begin ordered the attack because he feared Iraq was planning to use Osirak—a 40-megawatt plant, almost twice as powerful as Israel's Dimona facility—to manufacture plutonium for building an atomic bomb.[33]) To execute this raid, a force of six F-15s and eight F-16s traversed 600 miles of hostile territory undetected, violating Jordanian, Saudi Arabian, and Iraqi airspace. They pierced Iraqi air defenses that were on war alert (the Iraq-Iran conflict was still hot), destroyed Osirak, and, despite a heavy covering force of SAM-6 missiles and AA guns, escaped without loss.[34] Unsurpassed EW avionics and combat qualities make Eagle and Falcon Israel's master air defense penetrators.

In connection with the Osirak raid, it is perhaps also noteworthy that the F-16 demonstrated an unprecedented degree of ground-attack accuracy. Eight Falcons delivered all of their sixteen gravity bombs directly into the Osirak reactor's dome without a single miss.[35] Execution of this attack demanded extreme precision—delivery of the projectiles to within less than 100 feet of aimpoint—equivalent to the accuracy of cruise missiles or laser-guided munitions. Eagle, of similarly advanced design, must have the same pinpoint marksmanship. Such accuracy enables these aircraft to more effectively destroy enemy SAMs, AA guns, and radars, which means improved chances for successful air defense penetration. Furthermore, unlike other aircraft that are considered suitable only for making countercity atomic attacks, Falcon and Eagle probably are sufficiently accurate to perform nuclear strikes against both cities and the hardest forts, shelters, and other point targets.

The F-15 and F-16 outclass their rivals in penetration skill. Phantom was designed for carrying nuclear payloads in a penetrator role and is also a good bomber candidate. The F-4 can fly long distances at low altitudes, as low as 300 feet, to avoid radar detection and it carries EW equipment that performs many functions similar to those provided by F-15 and F-16. Although Phantom is not very maneuverable, it has an excellent dogfight record and is, in fact, one of the most successful aerial combat jets in history. But the F-4 is an old aircraft design that is now technologically outmoded and is not comparable in maneuverability, avionics, or combat qualities to Eagle or Falcon. Kfir is more maneuverable than Phantom and may be comparable in dogfight characteristics, but it cannot outfight the F-15 or the F-16. Kfir avionics are not as advanced, nor are they as comprehensive, as those available on Phantom. Skyhawk is inferior to Phantom, Eagle, and Falcon on all counts. In the penetration category, then, the F-15 and the F-16 are Israel's best choices for a nuclear bomber.

Nuclear Bomber Candidates: Range Compared

The IAF will want a nuclear delivery vehicle that can fly long distances to maximize the number of objectives it can attack. Figure 3.2 compares the combat radii for Israel's five bomber candidates and shows some of the targets they can and cannot reach. The combat radius of an aircraft varies with payload, fuel capacity and altitude. The radii given here assume that each jet is carrying maximum payload and fuel and following a high-low flight path. The radii also assume that no airborne refueling occurs. (Of course, all of the bomber candidates presented here could reach any of the cities shown, provided they are refueled often enough. Skyhawk, for example, can replenish itself from companion jets and, if sent on a mission accompanied by other A-4s, can feed off their reserves and easily increase its range.[36]) The Israelis, if given a choice between two aircraft equal in every other respect, would prefer the one that does not require refueling in order to reach its objective. Refueling complicates a mission and increases the risk of failure—tankers might be shot down by the enemy; bombers and tankers may fail to rendezvous; bombers and tankers may be detected by radar and intercepted as they rise to high altitude to link up (fuel transfer cannot be performed safely while cruising below radar). Any of these events could preclude mission success; therefore, in addition to having penetration capability, the Israelis would want their nuclear bomber to be able to fly the farthest distance possible on its own reserves, without refueling.

As Figure 3.2 shows, the F-15 can, without refueling, project a nuclear weapon the farthest distance—over twice as far as F-16, Kfir, and Skyhawk and nearly one-third again as far as Phantom. Eagle can strike Tehran (Iran) in the east; Riyadh, Mecca (Saudi Arabia), and Khartoum (Sudan) in the south; beyond Bengasi almost to Tripoli (Libya) in the west; and northward to Odessa, Rostov, and Baku in

Figure 3.2   The range of Israeli nuclear bombers. The outermost circle demarks the range of an F-15 flying a one-way mission. The inner circles indicate the ranges of various aircraft flying round-trip missions. Range estimates assume that each jet is carrying maximum payload.

the USSR. The F-15 enables Israel to attack its most distant actively hostile enemies.

Phantom is, by over 200 miles, the second best delivery vehicle for distance. Aside from the F-15, the F-4 is the only other jet in the IAF that can execute, without refueling, a round-trip nuclear mission against Libya. Unlike its F-16 rival, Phantom can reach most of the major cities of the two most militarily powerful Arab nations in the Middle East—Egypt and Iraq. Where range is the primary consideration, the bomber candidates Falcon and Kfir are distinctly tertiary choices. Skyhawk is last choice.

Range and Penetration Capabilities Against the USSR

It should be noted that the ranges given here are idealized in that they assume the jets can penetrate enemy air defenses and maintain a continuously straight flight path. In an actual war, neither of these capabilities is guaranteed, especially when flying against the USSR. Israeli jets flying against targets in the Middle East or Africa very likely can penetrate along a more or less straight line. But it is, in Harkavy's words, "most problematic" whether the Israelis can pierce "even the remote southern arc of the U.S.S.R."[37] Describing the difficulties involved in attacking the Soviet Union, Harkavy says:

> Aircraft flying toward the U.S.S.R. during a crisis would have to overfly long stretches (depending on their routes) of Arab, Iranian, Turkish, or Greek territory, while even low-profile flights over the Black Sea would be easily detectable by radar without the masking of ground terrain features and terrestrial clutter. Beyond that, the literally thousands of Soviet interceptors located along the periphery of the U.S.S.R. would be alerted and the very dense SAM belt around the Black Sea littoral would be most formidable obstacles.[38]

For these reasons, the Soviet targets specified in Figure 3.2 (especially those within the outermost circle representing F-15's maximum one-way flying distance) may not be accessible to the IAF. "Still," Harkavy insists, "it is not inconceivable that Israel could develop a minimally credible deterrent" capable "of reaching the U.S.S.R. with a small number of delivery systems in the event of extreme crisis."[39]

Although a nuclear strike against the Soviet Union might be most unlikely to succeed, at least Eagle has, without the added tactical encumbrance of refueling, some chance of executing a round-trip bombing run. Assuming that deep penetration is possible, on a one-way mission, F-15 Eagle could conceivably penetrate very deeply indeed: perhaps as far as Moscow itself. Phantom, Falcon, and Kfir, unrefueled, could reach only the southern extremities of the Soviet Union, and then only on a one-way suicide mission. Without refueling, Skyhawk cannot attack the USSR. Thus, where range is the primary concern, Eagle is the best choice for executing an atomic attack against the USSR or against any other potential enemy of Israel.

Israel's Best Nuclear Bomber

The F-15 Eagle is Israel's best aircraft overall for serving as a nuclear bomber. F-15 electronic warfare avionics and its penetration

The F-15 Eagle. (*Courtesy of David Rubinger,* Time Magazine.)

capabilities are equalled only by F-16; and Eagle offers far more range than any other jet, including F-16. It is also noteworthy that Eagle's payload capacity is matched only by Phantom. The ability to carry greater weight means that the F-15 can mount more defensive weaponry to fend off interceptors and that the burden of the bomb will exert less effect on Eagle's maneuverability and speed than it might on other jets. The F-15 is unsurpassed in the decisive categories of penetration and range and would probably be Israel's first choice for executing a nuclear mission.

Phantom and F-16 would be secondary choices. Before the Israelis purchased Eagle and Falcon, Phantom most likely was their preferred atomic bomber, as was allegedly evidenced in 1968 when they unsuccessfully attempted to buy nuclear bomb racks for the F-4 from the United States.[40] Phantom can fly farther than Falcon, but the IAF probably would choose the F-16 over the F-4 for striking targets within Falcon's combat radius because of the former's superior design.

Kfir and Skyhawk are inferior to the other aircraft in most, if not all, respects. They would probably be used to deliver atomic weapons only if none of the other jets were available. But this does not preclude or make impossible their use as nuclear bombers. In the midst of another Arab-Israeli war, it is entirely plausible that all F-15s, F-16s, and Phantoms would be tied up executing conventional attacks, necessitating reliance on Kfir and Skyhawk for a nuclear mission. This apparently was the case in the October War, when the Israelis reportedly were contemplating the use of a mixed force of Kfirs and Phantoms to make nuclear strikes against the enemy.[41]

Israeli reliance on inferior aircraft for making nuclear attacks is a possibility, albeit a remote one. Should Israel decide to exercise its atomic option, however, Israel probably will choose its best candidate—the F-15 Eagle—to drop the bomb.

4
Conclusion

This book has attempted to reconstruct the history of Israel's development of atomic weaponry and to define the probable characteristics of Israel's nuclear arsenal. In summary, the Israelis began their atomic program in 1948, with the Israel Defense Minstry's exploration of the Negev Desert for uranium deposits. In the 1950s, the United States unwittingly aided their bid for the bomb when President Eisenhower's "Atoms for Peace" program provided training to Israeli nuclear scientists, which resulted in the construction of Israel's first reactor, near Nahal Soreq. But France, not the United States is believed to have been Israel's principal teacher and willing partner in the development of fission arms. During the late 1950s and early 1960s, France trained technicians, may have shared its nuclear blast data, and helped build Israel's main atomic research and development center at Dimona. The Israelis apparently decided to actually construct atomic weapons after the 1967 Six Day War, with deployment probably occurring between 1969 and 1973. They may have contemplated using the bomb in the 1973 October War.

The fact that the Israelis did not launch a preemptive nuclear attack against the Arabs to prevent their October offensive indicates that their nuclear strategy is based on deterrence. Israel's alleged preparedness to make an atomic counterattack after its armies seemed defeated suggests that it is indeed willing to employ nuclear force— but only to retaliate for aggression already committed, and then only in the last extreme, after all else fails.

Israel continues to hint unofficially at its possession of atomic arms while officially denying that such arms exist. This "deliberate ambiguity," evidently put forward to avoid alienating the United States and other allies hostile to proliferation, continues to be part of Israel's atomic strategy. Israeli ambiguity about their atomic status could also serve the purpose of giving Israel leverage over the United States when bargaining for military hardware. The unspoken threat that an insecure Israel might resort to the bomb may enable the

Israelis to coerce the United States into meeting most of their demands for conventional arms.

Israel's sabotaging of Arab atomic equipment, and especially its destruction in 1981 of Iraq's Osirak reactor, demonstrates that the protection of its regional monopoly in fission weapons is a definite component of Israel's nuclear policy. While the Israelis are determined to prevent the Arabs from "going nuclear," they are today allegedly working with Taiwan and South Africa on nuclear and rocketry projects and may be helping these nations acquire the A-bomb in exchange for scientific and material support of their own ongoing atomic program.

In defining the characteristics of Israel's atomic arsenal, this work does not focus exclusively on weapons but also examines Israel's scientific and industrial nuclear infrastructure. The main research establishments are at the Weizmann Institute, the Soreq Nuclear Research Center, and the Negev Nuclear Research Center. The Weizmann Institute, other university institutions, and the Soreq Center probably do peaceful research only and train physicists and engineers, some of whom undoubtedly later work for the military at the Negev Center.

Breeding of plutonium for bomb manufacture probably takes place at the Negev Center's Dimona reactor, with separation done in its hot labs. Dimona has the theoretical potential to produce 6 to 7.8 kilograms of plutonium every twelve months, or enough to make 0.75 to 1.5 bombs yearly (depending upon whether 8 or 5 kilograms of Pu-239 are used in each device to achieve critical mass). These arms may be stored in an underground tunnel located at or near the Dimona reactor. The bombs may be kept "screw-ready" and 78 hours may be required for their assembly.

The A-bombs are most likely plutonium-based and implosion-configured, though there may well be a smaller number of weapons built from stolen uranium. Israel probably cannot enrich uranium to provide itself with a continuous supply for building bombs, so its nuclear weapons expertise is probably oriented toward plutonium-implosion designs. Consequently, the Israelis can be expected to face additional difficulties if they try to miniaturize warheads below 1,000 pounds for small missile and artillery delivery and to face fewer difficulties if they try to develop high-yield fission (over 200 kilotons) or fusion bombs, than would be the case if their weapons were uranium-based and gun-configured. Regardless of which design option is used, it is doubtful that Israel can make rapid progress in any of these areas because of its abstinence from atomic testing.

The evidence is too ambiguous to allow for an exact definition of certain critical characteristics of Israel's nuclear arsenal, specifically as regards bomb numbers, miniaturization, and delivery vehicles. Despite the ambiguity, these features can be defined to a narrow range by estimating the minimum and maximum probable quality of the arsenal. The minimum quality arsenal comprises those weapon capabilities that we can be virtually certain Israel has achieved or surpassed. The maximum quality arsenal comprises the most advanced weapon capabilities that can be credited to Israel and still remain, if just, in the realm of the probable.

At minimum, Israel almost certainly now has eleven plutonium A-bombs of some 20-kilotons yield. Almost certainly, the bombs weigh no more than 9,000 to 10,000 pounds apiece. Since evidence for advanced warhead miniaturization is rather ambiguous, an Israeli missile delivery capability cannot be claimed as virtually certain. Nuclear delivery can be performed by F-15 Eagle, with F-4 Phantom, and F-16 Falcon the next best choices.

At maximum, Israel probably now has thirty-one plutonium and ten uranium A-bombs, the latter assembled from stolen material. Israel probably can build weapons of widely different power with yields varying from 10 to perhaps as high as 200 kilotons. Nonetheless, their preference most likely is for the lower kiloton range. The Israelis probably can build miniaturized weapons weighing as little as 1,000 pounds and so can project warheads via the Jericho and Lance missiles, but not by small rockets or artillery. Israel's elite nuclear delivery vehicle is the F-15 Eagle. (Table 4.1 summarizes the minimum and maximum estimates in a more convenient form.)

It should once again be noted that the characteristics of Israel's nuclear arsenal given here are only educated guesses based on the best available evidence. Harkavy says, "All . . . assumptions" pertaining to Israel's atomic weaponry "are open to serious question because of technical factors that allow for variations in key parameters and because any or all assumptions may be simply incorrect."[1] He observes further that "extreme caution" should therefore be exercised "in drawing conclusions concerning Israel's present and potential nuclear capacity."[2] Harkavy is, of course, correct.

Some will be critical of this study for committing itself to specific figures and hard conclusions when everything about Israel's atomic status is still clouded in uncertainty. However, the extreme volatility of the Middle East demands that political and military assessments of possible future developments in that region take account of Israel's nuclear option. No discussion of Israeli strategic options can proceed without first defining the sophistication, power, range, and other

TABLE 4.1. Israel's Nuclear Arsenal: Minimum and Maximum Quality Estimated, January 1984

Estimate	Design	Weight (pounds)	Number	Yield (kilotons)	Storage Location	Delivery Vehicles
Minimum	Pu-239 fueled Implosion	3500-10,000	11[a]	20[a]	Unknown, but Dimona reactor or vicinity likely.	Aircraft exclusively. F-15 Eagle best choice
Maximum	Pu-239 fueled U-235 fueled Implosion Some gun	1000-2000	31[b] +10 / 41	10[b]	Unknown, but Dimona reactor or vicinity likely.	Aircraft, Jericho and Lance missiles. F-15 Eagle best choice

[a]Number assumes 8 kgs of Pu-239 per bomb out of 90 kgs available for eleven bombs. Yield assumes 8 kgs (17.6 lbs) fuel, bomb efficiency 15% to produce (at rate of 8 kts per 1 lb of plutonium burned) about 20 kilotons.

[b]Number (Pu-239) assumes 5 kgs of fuel per bomb out of 156 kgs available for thirty-one bombs. Yield (Pu-239) assumes 5 kgs (11 lbs) fuel, bomb efficiency 15%, to produce about 10 kilotons. Number (U-235) assumes 17 kgs of fuel per bomb out of 175.5 kgs available (stolen from NUMEC) for ten bombs. Yield (U-235) assumes 17 kgs (37.4 lbs) fuel, bomb (possible gun design) efficiency 3%, to produce about 10 kilotons.

characteristics of Israel's atomic weaponry. Thus, informed guesswork about Israel's nuclear capabilities is not only justified, but imperative.

Descriptions of Israel's atomic forces have been attempted in the past. These efforts, however, were generally superficial or uninformed and usually served only as an obligatory prelude to the author's main concern: analysis of the strategic and political implications of the Israeli A-bomb. Unfortunately, as a result, many analyses of tactical and strategic atomic capabilities have proceeded on incorrect assumptions about the probable nature of Israel's arsenal and have arrived at false conclusions. Other analyses have made much better, though still imperfect, assumptions about the probable characteristics of Israel's arsenal and have erred, when error could have been avoided had greater care been taken to first define arsenal characteristics. Major revisions may be required in many studies because of the conclusions presented here. One particularly significant example of this is evident in the "Rosen-Feldman thesis."

Steven Rosen, in his article "Nuclearization and Stability in the Middle East," cited earlier in this book, hypothesizes that, even if the Arabs eventually acquire the bomb, as long as Israeli atomic weapons remain invulnerable, the A-bomb may make the Middle East a less volatile place by creating a stable "balance of terror." Both sides will fear mutual destruction and refrain from aggression. More recently, Shai Feldman, in *Israeli Nuclear Deterrence* (1982), has developed in greater detail the same argument: that nuclear weapons can exert a positive stabilizing influence in the Middle East.[3] The Rosen-Feldman viewpoint, apparently now accepted by many defense experts, assumes that Israel can make miniaturized warheads suitable for delivery on missiles, which can be based in hardened silos and so protected from a disarming Arab surprise attack.

The "balance of terror" idea works only as long as Israeli nuclear forces are immune to attack, so that Israel has an assured ability to retaliate. But since Israel probably does not rely primarily upon missiles for delivery, owing to their too-limited range, and since it must use mainly aircraft for delivery, Israel's atomic forces are theoretically vulnerable to Arab nuclear or conventional surprise assault. Aircraft are not easy to protect. Because of the short distances between Arab and Israeli airfields (Syrian and Jordanian jets can reach most bases in less than ten minutes) and the proven ability of warplanes to elude radar detection, even when approaching from long distances (as the Israelis did against Iraq during the Osirak raid), the Arabs could deprive Israel of adequate early warning time and destroy Israel's nuclear bombers before they could get airborne. Jericho and Lance missiles are almost equally vulnerable because they are based, not in silos, but on mobile platforms easily monitored and difficult to conceal in Israel's open country. Even if the Israelis based their rockets in silos, the great accuracy of the newest aircraft and guided munitions would render their survival doubtful. Under these conditions, the Israelis would not possess a guaranteed capability to absorb an enemy surprise attack and to retaliate. Israel's nuclear second-strike would not be assured. Furthermore, as explained previously, even if Jericho and Lance survival could be guaranteed, these missiles would be an ineffective deterrent against such countries as Libya, Iraq, Iran, and the USSR because except for a sparsely inhabited corner of western Iraq, the missiles cannot reach these nations—the very parties most likely to pose a nuclear threat to Israel.

Even Feldman concedes that Israel's delivery system "appears to be a fairly vulnerable mix, particularly the aircraft and runways, which are useless without each other. It takes no more than two p.s.i. overpressure to destroy all parked aircraft. This raises a question of vulnerability to an Iraqi strike, since Iraq is outside the assumed range of Israel's Jerichos. A successful Iraqi nuclear attack against Israel's airfields would leave Israel unable to retaliate."[4] Feldman hopes that Israel can eliminate this vulnerability by developing a "surface to surface missile with sufficient range to reach Baghdad" and by acquiring VTOLs "to reduce dependency on runways."[5] But it is most unlikely that Israel can soon build a missile capable of reaching Baghdad (some 540 miles from Jerusalem), which would entail developing more powerful boosters and smaller warheads to almost double Jericho's range. (Historical precedent suggests that large-missile engineering is perhaps even a greater technical challenge than the A-bomb, as every member of the "nuclear club" armed with MRBMs or ICBMs had to invest more time and money on perfecting these systems than on the bomb itself.) The Israelis are not now testing any major rocket systems and cannot improve upon their current level of missile technology without a major program of launchings or upon their warhead miniaturization technology without performing detonations; and then the Baghdad rocket would still be years in prospect. Iraq will probably get the bomb before Israel acquires medium-range ballistic missiles that, as noted, may be no more survivable than aircraft anyway. As for VTOLs, they would be no better, no more survivable, than conventional jets. The primary problem with using aircraft for atomic delivery, especially if air bases are being subjected to nuclear strikes, is not runway vulnerability, but vehicle vulnerability.

Rosen and Feldman both appear to believe that the improbability that an Iraqi or Libyan surprise attack would be perfect, that all Israeli nuclear bombers would be destroyed, should be sufficient to deter an Arab attack since even a single Israeli A-bomb could inflict serious retaliatory damage. There are at least two rebuttals to this argument.

First, if the Arabs acquired enough bombs to hit all Israeli military airfields (there are ten) and perhaps a few more to destroy suspected A-bomb storage depots (the Soviets probably know where the weapons are kept), it is most unlikely that any delivery vehicles would survive. If an Arab nuclear first strike against Israel included destruction of key communication centers and assassination of key leaders, even if some bombs and delivery vehicles survived, the resulting disorganization and confusion would seem sufficient to prevent their being used for several hours at least, or long enough for the Arabs to launch a second attack to destroy the targets missed in their first strike. Even if all Israeli missiles survived a nuclear attack by Libya, Iraq, Iran, or some other similarly remote neighbor, Jericho and Lance lack sufficient range to retaliate effectively, or at all, against such distant nations.

Second, neither Rosen or Feldman seems to consider the possibility that, if the Arabs acquire the bomb, they could conduct surprise attacks against Israel's nuclear bombers and missiles using aircraft armed with conventional weapons. The Arab bomb could be held in reserve to deter Israeli nuclear retaliation, while Arab conventional forces attempt to destroy Israel's nuclear weaponry. This strategy could be employed even by Syria or Egypt or other nations within easy range of Jericho. Arab success in this scenario would not necessarily have to come in the initial assault, or swiftly. Even if some Israeli bombers survive the initial attack and get airborne, they must land for maintenance eventually—and Israel is a small nation vulnerable everywhere to strikes from the forward air bases (only a few minutes flying time away) of its neighbors. Victory could be achieved through slow attrition of Israel's nuclear delivery vehicles. On the other hand, the opposition, Syria and Egypt for example, has plenty of space far from Israel in which it can hide bombs and bombers, perhaps keeping them airborne and making periodic landings for maintenance at remote desert airstrips. Israel would find it difficult to monitor and attack enemy aircraft under these circumstances. The vulnerability of aircraft opens the very real possibility that the Arabs could disarm Israel's nuclear deterrent using conventional forces, while keeping their own weapons safe from attack, and thereby render Israel helpless to defend itself from the threat or actual use of Arab atomic bombs.

These circumstances tend to repudiate the Rosen-Feldman theory and support, instead, Amos Natan's view (articulated in *Israel-Arab States: Atom Armed or Atom Free?*) that atomic arms will further destabilize the Middle East, as nuclear forces, being mostly or exclusively aircraft delivered, cannot be protected and will be kept on a "hair trigger"—ready to strike on a moment's notice.[6] Crisis situations will tempt both sides to strike first, lest their enemy does so. Contrary to the argument of Rosen and Feldman, it would seem that the introduction of primarily jet-delivered A-bombs—not missile-delivered weapons, as they premised—onto both sides of the Middle Eastern equation would make war more likely.

Clearly, the probability that Israel's A-bombs must be projected mainly by aircraft, and not by rocket, has profound strategic ramifications. That Israel probably has no H-bombs or cruise missiles that can reach Moscow, as discussed earlier, is perhaps even more important strategically. The other characteristics of Israel's nuclear arsenal described here likewise have important strategic consequences. But exploring these consequences is beyond the scope of this book. It is hoped the conclusions presented here about the probable sophistication, number, power, readiness, and other features of Israeli atomic weaponry shall provide a basis for future updated analyses of the military capabilities of Israel's nuclear arsenal, and of its strategic and political implications, both for the Middle East and for the world.

Notes

Introduction

1. Robert J. Pranger and Dale R. Tahtinen, *Nuclear Threat in the Middle East* (Washington, DC: American Enterprise Institute for Public Policy Research, 1975), p. 50.

2. Victor Cohn, "Israel Says It Could Build Nuclear Weapons," *Washington Post* (3 December 1974), p. 13.

3. "Dayan Says Israelis Have the Capacity to Produce A-Bombs," *New York Times* (25 June 1981), p. 1.

4. Conversation with Shmuel Katz at the University of Southern California on 2 November 1983. In Kim Willenson, Lloyd H. Norman, Scott Sullivan, and Milan J. Kubic, "Israel: A Friend in Need," *Newsweek* (12 September 1977), p. 44, Katz is described as "Prime Minister Menachem Begin's closest advisor."

5. Fuad Jabber, *Israel and Nuclear Weapons: Present Options and Future Strategies* (London: Chatto & Windus, 1971).

6. David Binder, "C.I.A. Says Israel Has 10–20 A-Bombs," *New York Times* (16 March 1976), p. 5.

7. See, for example, Pranger and Tahtinen, *Nuclear Threat in the Middle East*, pp. 23–37.

8. David K. Shipler, "Israel Bans a Book on Atomic 'Arsenal,' " *New York Times* (30 March 1980), p. 5. Other histories, of a journalistic bent, include Chapter ten, "How Israel Joined the South African Nuclear Club," in Zdenek Červenka and Barbara Roger's *The Nuclear Axis* (1978); Chapter three, "The Israeli Connection," in D. K. Palit and P.K.S. Namboodiri's *Pakistan's Islamic Bomb* (1979); and Chapter eight, "The Making of the Israeli Bomb," in Steve Weissman and Herbert Krosney's *The Islamic Bomb* (New York: Times Books, 1981).

Chapter 1

1. Fuad Jabber, *Israel and Nuclear Weapons: Present Options and Future Strategies* (London: Chatto & Windus, 1971), p. 17; Robert E. Harkavy, *Spectre of a Middle Eastern Holocaust: The Strategic and Diplomatic Im-*

plications of the Israeli Nuclear Weapons Program (Denver, CO: University of Denver for Monograph Series in World Affairs, 1977), p. 5.

2. Jabber, *Israel and Nuclear Weapons*, p. 17.

3. Simha Flapan, "Nuclear Power in the Middle East" (Part 1), *New Outlook*, Vol. 17 (July 1974), pp. 49–50; Sylvia K. Crosbie, *A Tacit Alliance: France and Israel from Suez to the Six Day War* (Princeton, NJ: Princeton University Press, 1974), p. 55–56; and Jabber, *Israel and Nuclear Weapons*, pp. 17–19. Flapan, Crosbie, and Jabber all believe Ben-Gurion made the decision to develop an Israeli nuclear option by 1955. Jabber and Flapan both discuss in come detail the early years of the atomic program.

4. Jabber, *Israel and Nuclear Weapons*, pp. 25–27.

5. Ibid., p. 31.

6. Ibid., pp. 31–32.

7. Ibid., pp. 29, 31; U.S. Department of State, *United States Treaties and Other International Agreements*, Vol. 6, Pt. 2 (Washington, DC: GPO, 1956), pp. 2641–2646; "Israel Gets U.S. Atom Fuel," *New York Times* (4 March 1960), p. 11. Under the terms of the original treaty (see Department of State citation above), the United States was to supply Israel with uranium enriched to only 20% U-235. But when the Soreq reactor was completed, its design required, and the original treaty was changed on 20 August 1959 to allow for, the provision of fuel that was 90% enriched.

8. *Treaties and International Agreements Registered or Filed and Reported with the Secretariat of the United Nations*, United Nations Treaty Series, Vol. 573, No. 8320, pp. 4–20; U.S. Department of State, *United States Treaties and Other International Agreements*, Vol. 16, Pt. 2 (Washington, DC: GPO, 1966), pp. 1773–1774.

9. Harkavy, *Spectre of a Middle Eastern Holocaust*, p. 14; Tad Szulc, "Murder by Proxy," *Penthouse* (August 1975), p. 46.

10. Harkavy, *Spectre of a Middle Eastern Holocaust*, p. 14.

11. "Article Says Israel Got C.I.A. Atomic Aid," *New York Times* (12 July 1975), p. 11.

12. The United States did not begin officially to supply Israel with arms until the Johnson administration, the first sale being of HAWK missiles. Under Eisenhower, though military aid was supplied indirectly and from U.S. allies, Israel certainly must have understood that its past and future access to arms depended upon the good will of the United States, which was then stronger and more influential in its role as leader of the West.

13. Harkavy, *Spectre of a Middle Eastern Holocaust*, p. 14.

14. Ibid., p. 5; Crosbie, *A Tacit Alliance*, pp. 152–169; Jabber, *Israel and Nuclear Weapons*, p. 20. Jabber and Crosbie give the best accounts of French-Israeli nuclear cooperation. Jabber dates their "alliance" from 1953—the year in which the two nations signed an agreement calling for collaboration in the nuclear field.

15. Harkavy, *Spectre of a Middle Eastern Holocaust*, pp. 5–6; Jabber, *Israel and Nuclear Weapons*, pp. 20–22, 27; Crosbie, *A Tacit Alliance*, pp. 165–167; Steve Weissman and Herbert Krosney, *The Islamic Bomb* (New York: Times Books, 1981), p. 112.

16. William B. Bader, *The United States and the Spread of Nuclear Weapons* (New York: Pegasus for Center of International Studies, Princeton, 1968), pp. 33–35; Harkavy, *Spectre of a Middle Eastern Holocaust*, pp. 5–6.

17. Crosbie, *A Tacit Alliance*, pp. 167–168.

18. Ibid., p. 169 fn 42; Weissman and Krosney, *The Islamic Bomb*, pp. 113–115.

19. Pierre Gallois, *The Balance of Terror* (Boston: Houghton-Mifflin, 1961). Gallois argues that international stability may increase with an increased number of nuclear powers.

20. Harkavy, *Spectre of a Middle Eastern Holocaust*, p. 6.

21. Ernest W. Lefever, *Nuclear Arms in the Third World: U.S. Policy Dilemma* (Washington, DC: The Brookings Institution, 1979), p. 68; Jabber, *Israel and Nuclear Weapons*, pp. 22–23.

22. Weissman and Krosney, *The Islamic Bomb*, pp. 113, 74fn.

23. Simha Flapan, "Israel's Attitude Towards the NPT," in *Nuclear Proliferation Problems*, ed. Bhupendra Jasani (Cambridge, MA, London, and Stockholm: The MIT Press and Almqvist and Wiksell for SIPRI, 1974), pp. 276–277.

24. Robert J. Pranger and Dale R. Tahtinen, *Nuclear Threat in the Middle East* (Washington, DC: American Enterprise Institute for Public Policy Research, 1975), p. 12; Jabber, *Israel and Nuclear Weapons*, p. 41 fn 24; John W. Finney, "U.S. Misled at First on Israeli Reactor," *New York Times* (20 December 1960), p. 15.

25. Crosbie, *A Tacit Alliance*, pp. 165–166.

26. Jabber, *Israel and Nuclear Weapons*, p. 78.

27. Ibid.

28. Weissman and Krosney, *The Islamic Bomb*, p. 118.

29. Ibid., p. 112; Jabber, *Israel and Nuclear Weapons*, p. 35; J. C. Hurewitz, *Middle East Politics: The Military Dimension* (New York: Praeger, 1969), pp. 476–477. Hurewitz estimates the probable cost of the Dimona reactor to have been $75 million.

30. Lefever, *Nuclear Arms in the Third World*, p. 69.

31. Ibid.; *U.S. Foreign Policy and the Export of Nuclear Technology to the Middle East* (Hearings before the Subcommittee on International Organizations and Movements and on the Near East and South Asia of the House Committee on Foreign Affairs, 93rd Congress, 2nd Session, 1974), pp. 144–145 (cited in Lefever, *Nuclear Arms in the Third World*, p. 69 fn 23).

32. George Quester, "Implications of SALT Outcome for Potential 'Nth' Powers: Israel, India, and Others" (unpublished paper) (quoted in Harkavy, *Spectre of a Middle Eastern Holocaust*, p. 116 fn 8).

33. Jabber, *Israel and Nuclear Weapons*, p. 36; Harkavy, *Spectre of a Middle Eastern Holocaust*, pp. 6–7.

34. Hedrick Smith, "U.S. Assumes the Israelis Have A-Bomb or Its Parts," *New York Times* (18 July 1970), p. 8.

35. D. K. Palit and P.K.S. Namboodiri, *Pakistan's Islamic Bomb* (New Dehli: Vikas Publishing House, 1979), p. 49.

36. Smith, "U.S. Assumes the Israelis Have A-Bomb or Its Parts," p. 8; "Israel Bars U.S. Senators from A-Site," *Washington Post* (9 November 1976), p. 9.

37. Lefever, *Nuclear Arms in the Third World*, pp. 69–70.

38. Ibid., pp. 68–69.

39. Peter Braestrup, "France Will End Tests in Sahara," *New York Times* (16 March 1964), p. 6.

40. Harkavy, *Spectre of a Middle Eastern Holocaust*, pp. 26, 119 fn 2.

41. Samuel Glasstone, ed., *The Effects of Nuclear Weapons* (Washington, DC: GPO for U.S. Department of Defense and U.S. Atomic Energy Commission, 1962), p. 680.

42. Weissman and Krosney, *The Islamic Bomb*, pp. 112–113.

43. Ibid., p. 113.

44. Crosbie, *A Tacit Alliance*, pp. 159–161.

45. Ibid., pp. 159–160.

46. Ibid., p. 160.

47. Ibid.

48. Ibid.

49. Ibid., p. 159 fn 16; Jabber, *Israel and Nuclear Weapons*, p. 96.

50. Lefever, *Nuclear Arms in the Third World*, p. 66; Committee for Nuclear Disarmament, "Keep Nuclear Weapons Out of Our Region," *New Outlook*, Vol. 9 (July-August 1966), pp. 64–65; Eliezer Livneh, "Israel Must Come Out for Denuclearization," *New Outlook*, Vol. 9 (June 1966); Y. V., "Atoms and a Middle East Tashkent," *New Outlook*, Vol. 9 (March-April 1966), pp. 3–6; Yoram Nimrod and Amos Korczyn, "Suggested Patterns for Israeli-Egyptian Agreement to Avoid Nuclear Proliferation," *New Outlook*, Vol. 10 (January 1967). In 1966 and 1967, there appeared in Israel's press a spate of articles, many of them written by prominent Isreali atomic scientists, concerned with the dangers of nuclear proliferation in the Middle East. The timing of these works and their subject matter suggest that, during this period, Israel was drawing near to a fission weapon capability and may have been making the trasition from A-bomb research to A-bomb development. Particularly suggestive of this is the Committee for Nuclear Disarmament article. The article, really a declaration, was signed by dozens of nuclear physicists and engineers, many of them from the Weizmann Institute, and urged the "Knesset and government of Israel to take the political initiative . . . to prevent the proliferation of nuclear weapons in the Middle East." Most significantly, the declaration stated that if A-bombs, presumably Israeli, were to be kept out of the region, "the coming year or two are considered critical." Livneh, Y. V., and Nimrod and Korczyn also darkly hint that 1966-1967 was somehow an important transitional period for the Israeli atomic program and that a nuclear Middle East was imminent.

51. Joel Marcus, "The Rift Between Israel and France," *Midstream*, Vol. 14 (January 1968), pp. 39–44; Harkavy, *Spectre of a Middle Eastern Holocaust*, p. 7.

52. Harkavy, *Spectre of a Middle Eastern Holocaust*, pp. 8–9. Seymour Hersh, *Chemical and Biological Warfare* (Garden City, NY: Doubleday, 1969), pp. 244–247.

53. Harkavy, *Spectre of a Middle Eastern Holocaust*, p. 9; Avigdor Haselkorn, "Israel: From an Option to a Bomb in the Basement?" in *Nuclear Proliferation: Phase II,* ed. R. M. Lawrence and J. Larus (Lawrence, KS: University of Kansas Press, 1974), pp. 168–173 (cited in Harkavy, p. 117 fn 14).

54. "How Israel Got the Bomb," *Time,* Vol. 107 (12 April 1976), p. 39.

55. "Israel Said to Plan to Make Atom Bomb," *New York Times* (14 June 1967), p. 16.

56. Ibid.

57. Report of the Secretary General (U Thant), *The Effects of the Possible Use of Nuclear Weapons and on the Security and Economic Implications for States of the Acquisition and Further Development of These Weapons* (New York: United Nations, Department of Political and Security Council Affairs, 1968), p. 61; Jabber, *Israel and Nuclear Weapons,* p. 82. Jabber discusses the Thant Report in some detail.

58. Todd Friedman, "Israel's Nuclear Option," *Bulletin of the Atomic Scientists,* Vol. 30 (September 1974), p. 33; Trevor N. Dupuy, Grace P. Hayes, and John A. C. Andrews, *The Almanac of World Military Power* (London and New York: R. R. Bowker, 1974), p. 182; data on Israel's GNP and defense expenditures for the period from 1969 to 1973 can be found in the issues for these years of the International Institute for Strategic Studies' (IISS) annual publication *The Military Balance.*

59. Leonard Beaton, *Must the Bomb Spread?* (Harmondsworth, U.K.: Penguin Books for The Insitute for Strategic Studies, 1968), p. 78. Most articles and books that discuss Dimona's fuel consumption report the plant requires annually 24 tons of uranium fuel. (See, for example, Crosbie, *A Tacit Alliance,* p. 165; and Jabber, *Israel and Nuclear Weapons,* p. 89.) At least in Beaton and Jabber's case, this figure is derived from the assumption that Dimona's power is 24 megawatts and the formula that a natural uranium reactor consumes yearly one ton of uranium for every thermal megawatt of its generating capacity. Beaton and Jabber calculate from their premise about Dimona's generating capacity being 24 megawatts that the facility needs 24 tons of uranium fuel every year. However, W. B. Fisher, in *The Middle East and North Africa 1983–84* (London: Europa Publications, 1983), p. 399, lists Dimona's power as 26 MWt. If Dimona's power is 26 MWt, it might require 26 tons of uranium annually. Europa Publications, through personal correspondence, informed the author that the 26 MWt figure came from the IAEC itself.

60. Beaton, *Must the Bomb Spread?* p. 78; Jabber, *Israel and Nuclear Weapons,* p. 89.

61. Ibid.; Crosbie, *A Tacit Alliance,* p. 165.

62. Nicholas Valéry, "Israel's Silent Gamble with the Bomb," *New Scientist,* Vol. 64 (12 December 1974), p. 808; Jabber, *Israel and Nuclear Weapons,* pp. 89–91.

63. Elaine Davenport, Paul Eddy, and Peter Gillman, *The Plumbat Affair* (Philadelphia, PA: Lippincott, 1978); Weissman and Krosney, *The Islamic Bomb*, pp. 124–127.

64. Valéry, "Israel's Silent Gamble with the Bomb," p. 808.

65. Crosbie, *A Tacit Alliance*, p. 165.

66. Todd Friedman, "Israel's Nuclear Option," p. 31; Z. Ketzinel, "Uranium Sources, Production and Demand in Israel," *Peaceful Uses of Atomic Energy*, Vol. 8 (New York and Vienna: United Nations and International Atomic Energy Agency, 1972), pp. 8, 113–119; "Uranium in the Negev," *Jerusalem Post Weekly* (12 April 1972), cited in Friedman, p. 36, fns 7, 8. Ketzinel gives a very detailed account of Israel's uranium sources.

67. Jabber, *Israel and Nuclear Weapons*, p. 77.

68. Ibid.

69. Ibid.

70. Leonard Beaton, "Why Israel Does Not Need the Bomb," *New Middle East* (April 1969), pp. 7–11.

71. Crosbie, *A Tacit Alliance*, p. 169 fn 42.

72. "Tod aus der Textilfabrik," *Der Spiegel*, Vol. 23, No. 19 (5 May 1969), p. 148 (cited in Harkavy, *Spectre of a Middle Eastern Holocaust*, pp. 10, 117 fn 15.

73. Weissman and Krosney, *The Islamic Bomb*, pp. 113, 117–118.

74. Friedman, "Israel's Nuclear Option," p. 31; Leonard Beaton and John Maddox, *The Spread of Nuclear Weapons* (New York: Praeger for the Institute for Strategic Studies, 1962), p. 174.

75. Lefever, *Nuclear Arms in the Third World*, p. 70.

76. "How Israel Got the Bomb," p. 40.

77. Weissman and Krosney, *The Islamic Bomb*, pp. 108–109, 113.

78. Pranger and Tahtinen, *Nuclear Threat in the Middle East*, pp. 13–15.

79. Ibid.

80. Robert Gillette, "Uranium Enrichment: Rumors of Israeli Progress with Lasers," *Science*, Vol. 183 (22 March 1974), p. 1174.

81. Ibid.

82. Mason Willrich and Theodore B. Taylor, *Nuclear Theft: Risks and Safeguards* (Cambridge, MA: Ballinger Publishing Company, 1974), p. 18 (quoted in Pranger and Tahtinen, *Nuclear Threat in the Middle East*, p. 14 fn 26).

83. Harkavy, *Spectre of a Middle Eastern Holocaust*, pp. 26–27; Frank Barnaby, Jozef Goldblat, and Macha Levinson, *The NPT: The Main Political Barrier to Nuclear Weapon Proliferation* (London and New York: Taylor and Francis; and Crane, Russak & Company for Stockholm International Peace Research Institute, 1980), p. 4.

84. Harkavy, *Spectre of a Middle Eastern Holocaust*, p. 27.

85. Weissman and Krosney, *The Islamic Bomb*, pp. 120–123; Howard Kohn and Barbara Newman, "How Israel Got the Nuclear Bomb," *Rolling Stone*, No. 253 (1 December 1977), pp. 38–39; "Dayan Says Israelis Have the Capacity to Produce A-Bombs," *New York Times* (25 June 1981), pp. 1,

7; "Bomb-Rich Uranium Reported Lost," *New York Times* (24 August 1977), p. 14; Thomas O'Toole, "Lost Uranium Mystery," *Washington Post* (6 November 1977), p. 1; Deborah Shapley, "CIA Report Says Israel Secretly Obtained A-Matter," *Washington Post* (28 January 1978), p. 2; Thomas O'Toole, "CIA Repeats Fears on Missing Uranium," *Washington Post* (28 February 1978), p. 6.

86. Weissman and Krosney, *The Islamic Bomb*, p. 123.

87. Ibid., p. 121.

88. Ibid., p. 124.

89. Kohn and Newman, "How Israel Got the Nuclear Bomb," p. 38.

90. "Dayan Says Israelis Have the Capacity to Produce A-Bombs," p. 7.

91. United States Central Intelligence Agency, "Prospects for Further Proliferation of Nuclear Weapons" (memo dated 4 September 1974), p. 1 (quoted in Lefever, *Nuclear Arms in the Third World*, p. 65 fn 3).

92. Weissman and Krosney, *The Islamic Bomb*, p. 109.

93. Dale R. Tahtinen, *The Arab-Israeli Military Balance Today* (Washington, DC: American Enterprise Institute for Public Policy Research, 1973), p. 34.

94. Ibid.

95. Harkavy, *Spectre of a Middle Eastern Holocaust*, p. 9.

96. Lefever, *Nuclear Arms in the Third World*, pp. 65, 70.

97. Michael Getler, "A-Arms Believed in Egypt," *Washington Post* (21 November 1973), p. 1; *London Sunday Times* "Insight" Team, *The Yom Kippur War* (Garden City, NY: Doubleday, 1974), pp. 411–413 (cited in Harkavy, *Spectre of a Middle Eastern Holocaust*, pp. 12–13).

98. "How Israel Got the Bomb," p. 39.

99. Joseph Alsop, "An Israeli Threat," *Washington Post* (7 October 1974), p. 23.

100. Aubrey Hodes, "Implications of Israel's Nuclear Capability," *The Wiener Library Bulletin*, Vol. 22 (Autumn 1968); Fuad Jabber, "Not by War Alone: Curbing the Arab-Israeli Arms Race," *The Middle East Journal*, Vol. 28 (Summer 1974), p. 240; Yair Evron, "Israel and the Atom: The Uses and Misuses of Ambiguity, 1957–1967," *Orbis*, Vol. 17 (Winter 1974); Weissman and Krosney, *The Islamic Bomb*, p. 106.

101. Lefever, *Nuclear Arms in the Third World*, p. 75.

102. Steven J. Rosen, "Nuclearization and Stability in the Middle East," in *Nuclear Proliferation and the Near-Nuclear Countries*, ed. Onkar Marwah and Ann Schulz (Cambridge, MA: Ballinger Publishing Company, 1975), p. 157, passim; Louis René Beres, "Terrorism and the Nuclear Threat in the Middle East," *Current History*, Vol. 70–71 (January 1976), pp. 27–29. Beres notes that, in addition to Arab states, Middle Eastern terrorist organizations might also develop nuclear arms. It is hard to see how Rosen's "balance of terror" could work if subnational groups, having no base for Israel to threaten with nuclear retaliation, come into possession of the bomb.

103. "Possible Role of Mideast Agents in Toulon Reactor Blast Study," *New York Times* (14 April 1979), p. 4; Flora Lewis, "France Said to Pledge

to Replace Iraq-Bound Reactor," *New York Times* (9 May 1979), p. 3. These articles describe the sabotage of nuclear reactor equipment, bound for Iraq, which was stored in a guarded French warehouse at La Seyne. According to the first article, "This act of sabotage was the work of foreign secret agents, real professionals using highly sophisticated explosives and fuses." The articles do not specifically conclude that Israel was the culprit. But since the wrecked equipment was vital for completing Iraq's Osirak reactor, which the Israelis destroyed twenty-seven months later in an unprovoked air-strike, we can be sure that Israel was responsible for the deed.

104. Steven Strasser, "A Risky Nuclear Game," *Newsweek*, Vol. 97 (22 June 1981), pp. 20–21; Simha Flapan, "Nuclear Power in the Middle East," (Part 2), *New Outlook*, Vol. 17 (October 1974), pp. 36–37. The Osirak raid and acts of nuclear sabotage are not aberrations, wrought by the unusually aggressive Begin government, in Israel's normal behavior. Using force to preempt Arab technological ambitions has long been an aspect of Israel's policy. Flapan notes that during the early 1960s the Israelis conducted covert operations against Egypt's efforts to build a missile delivery system, which was being developed for the UAR by former Nazi rocket scientists. Israel attempted to derail Egypt's missile program by, among other things, assassinating the Germans.

105. M. S. Handler, "Adenauer to See Norstad Today in Preparation for Visit to U.S.," *New York Times* (21 May 1957), p. 10.

106. Zdenek Červenka and Barbara Rogers, *The Nuclear Axis: Secret Collaboration Between West Germany and South Africa* (New York: Times Books, 1978), p. 313.

107. Hedrick Smith, "Ulbricht Visit to Cairo Today Said to Have Been Urged by Soviet," *New York Times* (24 February 1965), p. 2.

108. Kohn and Newman, "How Israel Got the Nuclear Bomb," p. 38.

109. James F. Clarity, "Teheran Denies Plans to Use Atom Plant for Nuclear Arms," *New York Times* (29 May 1976), p. 5.

110. Kathleen Teltsch, "Egyptian at the U.N. Accuses Israelis of 'Nuclear Collusion' with South Africa and of Threatening Peace," *New York Times* (1 June 1978), p. 6.

111. Judith Miller, "3 Nations Widening Nuclear Contacts," *New York Times* (28 June 1981), p. 15.

112. Ibid.; "Taipei Denies Work on Atomic Weapons," *New York Times* (8 July 1975), p. 8; David Binder, "U.S. Finds Taiwan Develops A-Fuel," *New York Times* (30 August 1976), pp. 1, 4; Fox Butterfield, "Taiwan Denying Atomic Operation," *New York Times* (5 September 1976), p. 5; Jack Anderson, "3 Nations to Begin Cruise Missile Project," *Washington Post* (8 December 1980), p. B15; Robert E. Harkavy, "The Pariah State Sydrome," *Orbis,* Vol. 21, No. 3 (Fall 1977), pp. 646–648.

113. Miller, "3 Nations Widening Nuclear Contacts," p. 15, Jim Hoagland, "French Leader Confirms S. Africa Nuclear Ability," *Washington Post* (18 February 1977), p. 28; Jim Hoagland, "S. Africa, with U.S. Aid, near A-Bomb," *Washington Post* (16 February 1977), p. 12.

114. Kim Willenson, Lloyd H. Norman, Scott Sullivan, and Milan J. Kubic, "Israel: A Friend in Need," *Newsweek* (12 September 1977), p. 44.

115. Ibid.; "South Africa Says It Is Not Planning Atomic Bomb Tests," *New York Times* (22 August 1977), p. 3; John F. Burns, "Vorster Unequivocally Denies Nuclear Arms Program," *New York Times* (24 August 1977), p. 8. Vorster later denied that South Africa had any intention to test or develop atomic weapons. Foreign Minister Roelof F. Botha claimed that reports South Africa was about to perform an atomic test in the Kalahari, which was first publicly alleged by the Soviet news agency Tass, were Soviet propaganda aimed at further inflaming black African nations that were then holding an anti-apartheid congress in Lagos, Nigeria. See *New York Times* above.

116. Richard Burt, "Panel Doubts Flash Sighted off Africa Was Atomic," *New York Times* (15 July 1980), p. 9.

117. Barnaby, Goldblat, and Levinson, *The NPT*, p. 4.

118. Handler, "Adenauer to See Norstad Today in Preparation for Visit to U.S.," p. 10.

119. Jay Walz, "Nasser Exhibits Military Might," *New York Times* (24 July 1962), p. 6.

120. C. L. Sulzberger, "Foreign Affairs," *New York Times* (16 November 1963), p. 26.

121. David Ben-Gurion, *Israel: Years of Challenge* (New York: Holt, Rinehart and Winston, 1963) p. 208 (quoted in Weissman and Krosney, *The Islamic Bomb*, p. 111).

122. Sydney Gruson, "Wilson Proposes Nuclear-Free Zone in Mideast," *New York Times* (23 December 1964), p. 2.

123. John W. Finney, "U.S. Hears Israel Moves Toward A-Bomb Potential," *New York Times* (19 December 1960), p. 1.

124. "Cairo Editor Says Israel Plans to Test Nuclear Device Soon," *New York Times* (21 August 1965), p. 2.

125. James Feron, "Israelis Honor Atom Scientist," *New York Times* (14 May 1966), p. 3.

126. "Israeli Nuclear Deterrent Urged by Jerusalem Paper," *New York Times* (5 October 1968), p. 3.

127. Ibid.

128. Weissman and Krosney, *The Islamic Bomb*, p. 106.

129. Ibid.

130. "Ex-C.I.A. Aide Says Johnson Quashed Israel A-Bomb Data," *Washington Post* (2 March 1978), p. 18.

131. Smith, "U.S. Assumes the Israelis Have A-Bomb or Its Parts," p. 1.

132. United States Central Intelligence Agency, "Prospects for Further Proliferation of Nuclear Weapons," p. 1; David Burnham, "Ex–C.I.A. Man Says Johnson Heard in '68 Israel Had A-Bombs," *New York Times* (2 March 1978), p. 5.

133. Weissman and Krosney, *The Islamic Bomb*, p. 109; Binder, "C.I.A. Says Israel Has 10–20 A-Bombs," pp. 1, 5. It should be noted that the CIA later refused to confirm this estimate, apparently released accidentally by

Duckett, on the grounds that Israel's atomic status was too sensitive for public discussion. CIA director George Bush, however, unintentionally provided indirect confirmation of the estimate when he issued a statement accepting full responsibility for the disclosure of secret information at the briefing.

134. Lefever, *Nuclear Arms in the Third World*, p. 75.

135. "U.N. Panel Surveys Israeli Atom Skill," *New York Times* (9 July 1981), p. 6.

Chapter 2

1. Ernest W. Lefever, *Nuclear Arms in the Third World: U.S. Policy Dilemma* (Washington, DC: The Brookings Institution, 1979), pp. 68–69.

2. "How Israel Got the Bomb," *Time*, Vol. 107 (12 April 1976), pp. 39–40; *Wehrtechnik* (June 1976) quoted in Zdenek Červenka and Barbara Rogers, *The Nuclear Axis: Secret Collaboration Between West Germany and South Africa* (New York: Times Books, 1978), p. 318.

3. Richard Burt, "Panel Doubts Flash Sighted Off Africa Was Atomic," *New York Times* (15 July 1980), p. 9.

4. Steve Weissman and Herbert Krosney, *The Islamic Bomb* (New York: Times Books, 1981), p. 114.

5. Fuad Jabber, *Israel and Nuclear Weapons: Present Options and Future Strategies* (London: Chatto & Windus, 1971), p. 81.

6. Kim Willenson, Lloyd H. Norman, Scott Sullivan, and Milan J. Kubic, "Israel: A Friend in Need," *Newsweek* (12 September 1977), p. 44.

7. Thomas O'Toole and Marilyn Berger, "Tiniest A-Blasts Identifiable Now," *Washington Post* (11 April 1971), p. 1.

8. Ibid., pp. 1, 21.

9. Howard Morland, "The H-Bomb Secret," *The Progressive*, Vol. 43 (November 1979), pp. 20, 22.

10. Frank Barnaby, Jozef Goldblat, and Macha Levinson, *The NPT: The Main Political Barrier to Nuclear Weapon Proliferation* (London and New York: Taylor and Francis; and Crane, Russak & Company, for Stockholm International Peace Research Institute, 1980), p. 2; Theodore B. Taylor, "Commercial Nuclear Technology and Nuclear Weapon Proliferation," in *Nuclear Proliferation and the Near-Nuclear Countries*, ed. Onkar Marwah and Ann Schulz (Cambridge, MA: Ballinger Publishing Company, 1975), p. 116; Jabber, *Israel and Nuclear Weapons*, p. 71 fn 1.

11. Sharon Begley, John Carey, and Lynn Hall, "How to Build a Bomb," *Newsweek*, Vol. 97 (22 June 1981), p. 33; Barnaby, Goldblat, and Levinson, *The NPT*, p. 4; Taylor, "Commercial Nuclear Technology and Nuclear Weapon Proliferation," p. 116.

12. *World Armaments and Disarmament: SIPRI Yearbook 1977* (Cambridge, MA, and London: MIT Press; Almqvist and Wiksell, 1977), p. 22; Alexander De Volpi, *Proliferation, Plutonium and Policy: Institutional and Technological Impediments to Nuclear Weapons Propagation* (New York: Pergamon Press, 1979), pp. 84–85.

13. Barnaby, Goldblat, and Levinson, *The NPT*, pp. 2–4; Begley, Carey, and Hall, "How to Build a Bomb," p. 33.

14. Jabber, *Israel and Nuclear Weapons*, p. 72.

15. Ibid.

16. Ibid.

17. Ibid., pp. 72–73.

18. J. Beckman, "Gas Centrifuges for Cheaper Isotope Separation," in *Preventing the Spread of Nuclear Weapons*, ed. C. F. Barnaby (London: Souvenir Press for Pugwash Movement, 1969), p. 97 (cited in Jabber, *Israel and Nuclear Weapons*, p. 74 fn 9).

19. Barnaby, Goldblat, and Levinson, *The NPT*, p. 4.

20. Jabber, *Israel and Nuclear Weapons*, p. 74.

21. William Van Cleave, "Nuclear Technology and Weapons," in *Nuclear Proliferation: Phase II*, eds. Robert M. Lawrence and Joel Larus (Lawrence, KS: University of Kansas Press, 1974), p. 47.

22. *SIPRI Yearbook 1977*, p. 36.

23. Begley, Carey, and Hall, "How to Build a Bomb," p. 33.

24. Van Cleave, "Nuclear Technology and Weapons," p. 46.

25. Ferguson's report is cited in Thomas O'Toole, "Making Plutonium Held Easier Than Supposed," *Washington Post* (10 November 1977), p. 16. Another relevant article is Thomas O'Toole, "Magazine Says Israelis Hijacked A-Bomb Fuel," *Washington Post* (25 October 1977), p. 3. Both of these articles imply it is easier to manufacture plutonium than uranium for making fission explosives—another reason for thinking Israel has chosen the former route to the bomb.

26. Weissman and Krosney, *The Islamic Bomb*, pp. 108–109; Leonard Beaton, "Why Israel Does Not Need the Bomb," *New Middle East* (April 1969), pp. 7–11; Todd Friedman, "Israel's Nuclear Option," *Bulletin of the Atomic Scientists*, Vol. 30 (September 1974), p. 31. "Tod aus der Textilfabrik," *Der Spiegel*, Vol. 23, No. 19 (5 May 1969), p. 148; Robert E. Harkavy, *Spectre of a Middle Eastern Holocaust: The Strategic and Diplomatic Implications of the Israeli Nuclear Weapons Program* (Denver, CO: University of Denver for Monograph Series in World Affairs, 1977), p. 117 fn 15 says of the *Der Spiegel* report, "This article claimed the Israeli SP had a production output of only 6 kilograms per year, which . . . would be rather a bottleneck in the overall Israeli program, limiting it to a level below the available unseparated plutonium Dimona can produce."

27. Červenka and Rogers, *The Nuclear Axis*, p. 320.

28. *SIPRI Yearbook 1977*, pp. 8–9, 47, 48, 30; The claim by Červenka and Rogers that, according to SIPRI, Israel has a reprocessing plant and that "SIPRI data is that released and carefully screened by the Israel Atomic Energy Commission" (*The Nuclear Axis*, p. 320) is contradicted by their source. They make an unpaginated reference to *SIPRI Yearbook 1977*, presumably to support their statement, but a review of all SIPRI allusions to Israeli reprocessing capabilities fails to provide corroboration. SIPRI tables (pp. 8–9, 47), showing reprocessing plants in operation, under construction,

or planned worldwide, attribute no such facility to Israel—not even in the planning stage. Another table (p. 48) credits Israel with a reprocessing plant, but clearly indicates that the existence of the plant is only assumed, not known. Elsewhere SIPRI emphasizes that it is uncertain whether Israel possesses a reprocessing facility: "The French firm Saint Gobain Techniques Nouvelles assisted Israel in building its (assumed) reprocessing plant" (SIPRI's parentheses, p. 30). Nowhere does *SIPRI Yearbook 1977* claim IAEC as a source.

29. "How Israel got the Bomb," pp. 39–40; Lefever, *Nuclear Arms in the Third World*, p. 70; Weissman and Krosney, *The Islamic Bomb*, pp. 108–109, 113.

30. Lefever, *Nuclear Arms in the Third World*, p. 70.

31. U.S. Central Intelligence Agency, "Prospects for Further Proliferation of Nuclear Weapons" (memo dated 4 September 1974), p. 1.

32. David Ben-Gurion, *Israel: A Personal History* (New York: Funk and Wagnalls, 1971), p. 660.

33. Beaton, "Why Israel Does Not Need the Bomb," pp. 7–11; Friedman, "Israel's Nuclear Option," p. 31; Lefever, *Nuclear Arms in the Third World*, p. 70.

34. Robert Gillette, "U.S. Test Shows Nuclear Bombs Can Be Made from Low-Grade Plutonium," *Washington Post* (14 September 1977), p. 7.

35. Ibid.

36. Ibid.; Begley, Carey, and Hall, "How to Build a Bomb," p. 33. Begley, Carey, and Hall call the plutonium route "a more effective way to build a bomb" than via uranium.

37. Harkavy, *Spectre of a Middle Eastern Holocaust*, p. 26.

38. Morland, "The H-bomb Secret," p. 18; Victor K. McElheny, "The French Bomb: How much Technical Fallout?" *Science*, Vol. 147 (1 January 1965), p. 35. Most sources say that H-bombs use uranium, not plutonium, triggers. Morland, however, who describes H-bomb design in far more detail than anyone else, specifies that a plutonium trigger is used. McElheny indicates that French H-bombs utilize plutonium instead of uranium to initiate fission.

39. Bertrand Goldschmidt, *The Atomic Adventure: Its Political and Technical Aspects* (London and New York: Pergamon Press and Macmillan Company, 1964), p. 78; W. Granger Blaire, "France Explodes Her First A-Bomb in a Sahara Test," *New York Times* (13 February 1960), p. 1; Bernard Weinraub, "India Becomes 6th Nation to Set Off Nuclear Device," *New York Times* (19 May 1974), pp. 1, 18; "Peking Is Upgraded on Atom Technique," *New York Times* (22 October 1964), pp. 1, 3.

40. Sylvia K. Crosbie, *A Tacit Alliance: France and Israel from Suez to the Six Day War* (Princeton, NJ: Princeton University Press, 1974), p. 166. Crosbie is among the few who appear to believe that an Israeli fission device would be "most likely of U-235 design."

41. Harkavy, *Spectre of a Middle Eastern Holocaust*, p. 26.

42. Morland, "The H-bomb Secret," pp. 19–20; Begley, Carey, and Hall, "How to Build a Bomb," p. 33.

43. Harkavy, *Spectre of a Middle Eastern Holocaust*, p. 26.

44. U.S. Office of Technology Assessment (OTA), *Nuclear Proliferation and Safeguards* (New York: Praeger, 1977), p. 142.

45. Harkavy, *Spectre of a Middle Eastern Holocaust*, p. 26.

46. W. Davidon, M. Kalkstein, and C. Hohenemser, *The Nth Country Problem and Arms Control* (Washington, DC: National Planning Association, 1960); William Van Cleave, "Nuclear Technology and Weapons." (The above are cited in Harkavy as authorities on the design of nuclear weapons and, presumably, in support of his observations about A-bomb design. See Harkavy, *Spectre of a Middle Eastern Holocaust*, pp. 26, 119 fn 4.)

47. OTA, *Nuclear Proliferation and Safeguards*, p. 142; Van Cleave, "Nuclear Technology and Weapons," p. 52; Morland, "The H-bomb Secret," pp. 18–20. Morland describes the operation of an implosion fission device, for detonating an H-bomb, that uses both Pu-239 and U-235.

48. Morland, "The H-bomb Secret," p. 18.

49. Ibid.

50. "Peking Is Upgraded on Atom Technique," p. 3.

51. *Treaties and International Agreements Registered or Filed and Reported with the Secretariat of the United Nations*, United Nations Treaty Series, Vol. 573, No. 8320.

52. Jabber, *Israel and Nuclear Weapons*, p. 31.

53. *U.S. Foreign Policy and the Export of Nuclear Technology to the Middle East* (Hearings before the Subcommittee on International Organizations and Movements and on the Near East and South Asia of the House Committee on Foreign Affairs, 93rd Congress, 2nd Session, 1974), pp. 144–145 (cited in Lefever, *Nuclear Arms in the Third World*, p. 69 fn 23).

54. Jabber, *Israel and Nuclear Weapons*, p. 88.

55. Ibid.; James R. Schlesinger, "Nuclear Spread," *Yale Review*, Vol. 57 (Autumn 1967), p. 80.

56. Jabber, *Israel and Nuclear Weapons*, p. 88.

57. Ibid.; W. B. Fisher (ed.), *The Middle East and North Africa 1983–84* (London: Europa Publications, 1983), p. 399; Simon Holder (editor, *The Middle East and North Africa*), personal correspondence (4 July 1983). As noted earlier (see Chapter 1, fn 59) most authors, including Jabber, report the power of Dimona is 24 megawatts thermal. If Dimona's fission power is 24 Mwt, applying the formula $Pu_1 = MWt * D/1000$, the reactor can produce 7.2 kilograms of plutonium annually, or enough to build 0.9 to 1.4 A-bombs every year, depending upon whether 8 or 5 kilograms are used in each weapon. *The Middle East and North Africa 1983–84* and its predecessors, however, extending back to the 1970–71 edition, claim Dimona's power is really 26 MWt. Simon Holder of Europa Publications assures the author that Europa's 26 MWt figure "is supplied and checked by the Israel Atomic Energy Commission itself on an annual basis." This has been independently verified.

58. Jabber, *Israel and Nuclear Weapons*, p. 88. Jabber uses this formula for approximating the plutonium output of the reactor.

59. Van Cleave, "Nuclear Technology and Weapons," p. 41.

60. "Tod aus der Textilfabrik" (cited in Harkavy, *Spectre of a Middle Eastern Holocaust*, p. 117 fn 15); "How Israel Got the Bomb," pp. 39–40; Lawrence Freedman, "Israel's Nuclear Policy," *Survival*, Vol. 17 (May/June 1975), p. 115.

61. Thomas O'Toole, "Earlier Try of Indian Bomb Told," *Washington Post* (13 July 1974), p. 3.

62. Jabber, *Israel and Nuclear Weapons*, p. 71. Jabber defines "critical mass" as "the minimum amount of fissile material required in a particular configuration to sustain" a "chain reaction. If the critical mass is left 'uncontrolled,' the reaction will take place at very high speed and the mass will explode instantaneously, releasing vast amounts of energy."

63. Van Cleave, "Nuclear Technology and Weapons," p. 47.

64. Begley, Carey, and Hall, "How to Build a Bomb," p. 33.

65. O'Toole, "Making Plutonium Held Easier Than Supposed," p. 16.

66. Shyam Bhatia, *India's Nuclear Bomb* (Sahibabad, India: Vikas Publishing, 1979), pp. 104–105.

67. David Binder, "C.I.A. Says Israel Has 10–20 A-Bombs," *New York Times* (16 March 1976), p. 1; "U.N. Panel Surveys Israeli Atom Skill," *New York Times* (9 July 1981), p. 6.

68. Taylor, "Commercial Nuclear Technology and Nuclear Weapon Proliferation," p. 116.

69. Jabber, *Israel and Nuclear Weapons*, p. 88; Arnold Kramish, *The Peaceful Atom in Foreign Policy* (New York: Harper & Row for the Council on Foreign Relations, 1963), p. 21.

70. "U.N. Panel Surveys Israeli Atom Skill," p. 6.

71. Binder, "C.I.A. Says Israel Has 10–20 A-Bombs," p. 1.

72. "Bomb-Rich Uranium Reported Lost," *New York Times* (24 August 1977), p. 14.

73. "Israel Denies a Report It Tested Atom Bomb in the South Atlantic," *New York Times* (23 February 1980), p. 5; Shai Feldman, *Israeli Nuclear Deterrence: A Strategy for the 1980s* (New York: Columbia University, 1982), p. 1.

74. "Israeli Nukes," *Washington Post Parade Magazine* (12 April 1981), p. 27; Robert D. McFadden, "Rolling Stone Magazine Says Israelis Stole Uranium for Nuclear Arms," *New York Times* (25 October 1977), p. 8. McFadden reports that Kohn and Newman "said at a news conference . . . that a Central Intelligence Agency estimate that Israel had 15 nuclear bombs was conservative and that they had confirmed reports of up to 150 bombs." Curiously, Kohn and Newman do not repeat this claim in their article "How Israel Got the Nuclear Bomb," which was published after the news conference.

75. "Israel Denies a Report It Tested Atom Bomb in the South Atlantic," p. 5.

76. Ibid.

77. Weissman and Krosney, *The Islamic Bomb*, p. 110.

78. *The Arms Trade and the Third World* (New York: Humanities Press for Stockholm International Peace Research Institute, 1971), p. 781; Harkavy, *Spectre of a Middle Eastern Holocaust*, p. 26.

79. Samuel Glasstone (ed.), *The Effects of Nuclear Weapons* (Washington, DC: GPO for U.S. Department of Defense and U.S. Atomic Energy Commission, 1962), p. 5.

80. De Volpi, *Proliferation, Plutonium and Policy*, p. 85.

81. The Committee for the Compilation of Materials on Damage Caused by the Atomic Bombs in Hiroshima and Nagasaki, *Hiroshima and Nagasaki*, translated by Eisei Ishikawa and David Swain (New York: Basic Books, 1981), p. 30; Frank Barnaby, "The Continuing Body Count at Hiroshima and Nagasaki," *Bulletin of the Atomic Scientists*, Vol. 33 (December 1977), p. 49; De Volpi, *Proliferation, Plutonium and Policy*, p. 85.

82. See, for example: Steven J. Rosen, "Nuclearization and Stability in the Middle East," in *Nuclear Proliferation and the Near-Nuclear Countries*, ed. Onkar Marwah and Ann Schulz (Cambridge, MA: Ballinger Publishing Company, 1975), p. 166; "How Israel Got the Bomb," p. 39; Nicholas Valéry, "Israel's Silent Gamble with the Bomb," *New Scientist*, Vol. 64 (12 December 1974), p. 807; Dale R. Tahtinen, *The Arab-Israeli Military Balance Today* (Washington, DC: American Enterprise Institute for Public Policy Research, 1973), p. 34; Freedman, "Israel's Nuclear Policy," p. 114; Harkavy, *Spectre of a Middle Eastern Holocaust*, p. 25.

83. Rosen, "Nuclearization and Stability in the Middle East," p. 166. For the yield of the first A-bomb explosions by the several nuclear nations, see: Glasstone, *The Effects of Nuclear Weapons*, pp. 672, 680 (United States and France); "Bomb Called '45 Type," *New York Times* (8 November 1949), p. 20; (USSR); John W. Finney, "China Tests Atomic Bomb, Asks Summit Talk on Ban: Johnson Minimizes Peril," *New York Times* (17 October 1964), p. 1; Weinraub, "India Becomes 6th Nation to Set Off Nuclear Device," pp. 1, 18.

84. Van Cleave, "Nuclear Technology and Weapons," p. 53.

85. Shai Feldman, of the Center for Strategic Studies at Tel Aviv University, thinks the yield of Israeli A-bombs could range from 20 to 60 kilotons, the high figure coming, presumably, from the fact that France's first explosion measured some 60 to 70 kilotons. See: Feldman, *Israeli Nuclear Deterrence*, p. 1.

86. Richard Halloran, "U.S. Holds off on Neutron Bomb; Some Officers Hail French Test," *New York Times* (28 June 1980), pp. 1, 5; James Gerstenzang, Untitled, *New York Times* (19 October 1978), p. 5: no author, Untitled, *New York Times* (20 October 1978), p. 83.

87. "Dayan Says Israelis Have the Capacity to Produce A-Bombs," *New York Times* (25 June 1981), p. 7.

88. "How Israel Got the Bomb," p. 39.

89. Ibid.

90. Ibid.

91. Arthur Kramish, "CIA: Israel Has 10–20 A-Weapons," *Washington Post* (15 March 1976), p. 2; Binder, "C.I.A. Says Israel Has 10–20 A-Bombs," p. 1.

92. Victor Cohn, "Israel Says It Could Build Nuclear Weapons," *Washington Post* (3 December 1974), p. 13.

93. Weissman and Krosney, *The Islamic Bomb*, pp. 106–107.

94. "How Israel Got the Bomb," p. 39.

95. Ibid.

96. David K. Shipler, "Israelis Are Critical of U.S. Decision to Hold Up F-17s for Raid on Iraq," *New York Times* (12 June 1981), p. 1.

97. Crosbie, *A Tacit Alliance*, pp. 162–163.

98. Aubrey Hodes, "Implications of Israel's Nuclear Capability," *The Wiener Library Bulletin*, Vol. 22 (Autumn 1968), p. 33 fn 1.

99. *Wehrtechnik* (June 1976), quoted in Červenka and Rogers, *The Nuclear Axis*, p. 318; "How Israel Got the Bomb," p. 40.

100. "Montreal Paper Asserts Israel Has Atomic Bombs," *New York Times* (8 May 1969), p. 15; Abba Eban, *Abba Eban: An Autobiography* (New York: Random House, 1977), p. 490; "How Israel Got the Bomb," p. 40.

Chapter 3

1. Robert J. Pranger and Dale R. Tahtinen, *Nuclear Threat in the Middle East* (Washington, DC: American Enterprise Institute for Public Policy Research, 1975), pp. 27–37. "Jericho" has also been called the "MD-620."

2. Steven J. Rosen, "Nuclearization and Stability in the Middle East," in *Nuclear Proliferation and the Near-Nuclear Countries*, ed. Onkar Marwah and Ann Schulz (Cambridge, MA: Ballinger Publishing Company, 1975), p. 165.

3. Gladwin Hill, "Cannon Fires Atomic Shell: Target 7 Miles Away Blasted," *New York Times* (26 May 1953), pp. 1, 18.

4. Evidence that the United States had to make a major effort to invent miniature warheads can be found in: Stewart Alsop and Ralph Lapp, "Can the New A-Bomb Stop Troops in the Field?" *Saturday Evening Post,* Vol. 224, Pt. 1 (29 September 1951); "Big Ones & Little Ones," *Time,* Vol. 58, Pt. 2 (15 October 1951), p. 22; "Atomic Artillery Tests," *Newsweek,* Vol. 38, Pt. 2 (22 October 1951), pp. 25–26.

5. Samuel Glasstone (ed.), *The Effects of Nuclear Weapons* (Washington, DC: GPO for U.S. Department of Defense and U.S. Atomic Energy Comission, 1962), pp. 672–673.

6. Articles pertaining to France's first deployment of a missile armed with nuclear warheads are: Henry Tanner, "French Hint Plan to Build ICBMs," *New York Times* (28 February 1968), p. 7; Henry Giniger, "$16.7 Billion Military Program Is Approved by Paris Deputies," *New York Times* (10 October 1970), p. 3; "Nuclear Missile Trucks Shown at Bastille Day Parade," *New York Times* (15 July 1970), p. 3.

For a record of French nuclear tests between 1960 and 1970, see the following issues and pages of *The New York Times*: 13 February 1960, p.

1; 1 April 1960, p. 1.; 27 December 1960, p. 6; 25 April 1961, p. 1.; 8 May 1962, p. 1; 24 October 1963, p. 3; 24 February 1964, p. 4; 8 December 1964, p. 8; 2 July 1966, p. 22; 12 September 1966, p. 22; 25 September 1966, p. 22; 5 October 1966, p. 3; 6 June 1967, p. 41; 28 June 1967, p. 4; 3 July 1967, p. 15; 8 July 1968, p. 4; 16 July 1968, p. 7; 4 August 1968, p. 29; 25 August 1968, p. 1; 9 September 1968, p. 18; 16 May 1970, p. 5; 23 May 1970, p. 3; 31 May 1970, p. 9; 25 June 1970, p. 7; 4 July 1970, p. 7; 28 July 1970, p. 15; 3 August 1970, p. 11.

7. Ciro E. Zoppo, "The Nuclear Genie in the Middle East," *New Outlook*, Vol. 18 (February 1975), p. 24; Augustus R. Norton, "Nuclear Terrorism and the Middle East," *Military Review*, Vol. 56 (April 1976), p. 10. Norton says, "The configuration of missile warheads or nuclear artillery rounds is dismissed out-of-hand as beyond the capability of the fledgling bomb manufacturer."

8. Nicholas Valéry, "Israel's Silent Gamble with the Bomb," *New Scientist*, Vol. 64 (12 December 1974), p. 809.

9. Ibid.

10. "Baby Bombs," *Time*, Vol. 55, Pt. 2 (22 May 1950), p. 69; Glasstone, *The Effects of Nuclear Weapons*, p. 672.

11. "Paris Announces Improved A-Bombs," *New York Times* (13 July 1965), p. 1; *London Sunday Times* "Insight" Team, *The Yom Kippur War* (Garden City, NY: Doubleday, 1974), p. 283 (quoted in Rosen, "Nuclearization and Stability in the Middle East," p. 181 fn 32). See Chapter 3, footnote 6 in these notes for a record of French bomb tests conducted between 1960 and 1965.

12. C. L. Mader, *Detonation Properties of Condensed Explosives* (Los Alamos: Los Alamos Scientific Laboratory, February 1963), LA-2900; J. H. Tillotson, *Metallic Equations of State for Hypervelocity* (Gulf General Atomic), GA-3216; H. C. Paxton, *Critical Dimensions of Systems Containing U-235, Pu-239, U-233* (Los Alamos: Los Alamos Scientific Laboratory, June 1964), TID-7028.

13. William Van Cleave, "Nuclear Technology and Weapons," in *Nuclear Proliferation: Phase II*, eds. Robert M. Lawrence and Joel Larus (Lawrence, KS: University of Kansas Press, 1974), p. 53.

14. Louis René Beres, *Apocalypse: Nuclear Catastrophe in World Politics* (Chicago and London: University of Chicago Press, 1980), pp. 7–8 fn 6.

15. Van Cleave, "Nuclear Technology and Weapons," p. 53.

16. Fuad Jabber, *Israel and Nuclear Weapons: Present Options and Future Strategies* (London: Chatto & Windus, 1971), p. 96; Rosen, "Nuclearization and Stability in the Middle East," p. 168.

17. Ernest W. Lefever, *Nuclear Arms in the Third World: U.S. Policy Dilemma* (Washington, DC: Brookings Institute, 1979), p. 65.

18. Clarence A. Robinson, Jr., "Lance Delivery to Israel Expected Soon," *Aviation Week & Space Technology*, Vol. 102 (17 February 1975), p. 46; James E. Dornan, Jr., "Tactical Nuclear Weapons and US Military Capabilities," in *The US War Machine*, ed. Ray Bonds (New York: Crown Publishers, 1983), p. 88.

19. Mark Heller, Dov Tamari, and Zeev Eytan, *The Middle East Military Balance 1983* (Tel Aviv, Israel: *The Jerusalem Post* for Tel Aviv University and Jaffee Center for Strategic Studies, 1983), p. 117.

20. Sylvia K. Crosbie, *A Tacit Alliance: France and Israel from Suez to the Six Day War* (Princeton, NJ: Princeton University Press, 1974), pp. 158–159.

21. Robert E. Harkavy, *Spectre of a Middle Eastern Holocaust: The Strategic and Diplomatic Implications of the Israeli Nuclear Weapons Program* (Denver, CO: University of Denver for Monograph Series in World Affairs, 1977), pp. 34–35; Hedrick Smith, "U.S. Assumes Israelis Have Atomic Bomb or Its Parts," *New York Times* (18 July 1970), p. 8; Jabber, *Israel and Nuclear Weapons*, p. 96.

22. Heller, Tamari, and Eytan, *The Middle East Military Balance 1983*, pp. 115, 117.

23. Smith, "U.S. Assumes Israelis Have Atomic Bomb or Its Parts," p. 8; Crosbie, *A Tacit Alliance*, p. 159 fn 16.

24. Crosbie, *A Tacit Alliance*, p. 160; Smith, "U.S. Assumes Israelis Have Atomic Bomb or Its Parts," p. 8; William Beecher, "Watch on Suez: Israel Weighs Options," *Army*, Vol. 21 (December 1971), p. 31; Dale R. Tahtinen, *The Arab-Israeli Military Balance Today* (Washington, DC: American Enterprise Institute for Public Policy Research, 1973), p. 33.

25. Lewis A. Dunn, *Controlling the Bomb: Nuclear Proliferation in the 1980s* (New Haven and London: Yale University Press, 1982), p. 39; "Israeli Nukes," *Washington Post Parade Magazine* (12 April 1981), p. 27 (cites *Foreign Report*); Jack Anderson, "3 Nations to Begin Cruise Missile Project," *Washington Post* (8 December 1980), p. B15.

26. Harkavy, *Spectre of a Middle Eastern Holocaust*, pp. 37–38; George Quester, "The Politics of Twenty Nuclear Powers," in *The Future of the International Strategic System,* ed. Richard Rosecrance (San Francisco: Chandler, 1972), pp. 56–77; Norton, "Nuclear Terrorism and the Middle East," p. 10. Quester and Norton agree with Harkavy that a fledgling nuclear power might rely on exotic means, like cargo planes and other unconventional vehicles, to effect delivery.

27. Terence Smith, "Jet Crash-Lands," *New York Times* (22 February 1973), p. 1.

28. Menachem Begin, *The Revolt* (New York: Nash Publishing, 1977), p. 209.

29. *The Military Balance 1981–1982* (London: The International Institute for Strategic Studies, 1981), p. 52.

30. Valéry, "Israel's Silent Gamble with the Bomb," p. 809.

31. John W. R. Taylor (ed.), *Jane's All The World's Aircraft 1980–1981* (London: Jane's Publishing Company, 1980), pp. 381–383, 345–347.

32. Valéry, "Israel's Silent Gamble with the Bomb," p. 809.

33. There is some disagreement about the megawattage of Iraq's reactor. Early reports (see, for example, Sharon Begley, John Carey, and Lynn Hall, "How to Build a Bomb," *Newsweek*, Vol. 97 [22 June 1981], p. 33) placed

its power at 70 megawatts. Bertrand Barre, the chief nuclear attaché of the French embassy in Washington, later indicated that this figure, widely circulated in the press, was wrong. The real power of Osirak, according to Barre, was 40 megawatts. This estimate should be used since France designed and was constructing the Iraqi facility. For Barre's correction, see: Judith Miller, "Senators Skeptical of Israeli Argument," *New York Times* (17 June 1981), p. 6.

34. Angus Deming, Milan J. Kubic, and Ron Moreau, "Two Minutes over Baghdad," *Newsweek*, Vol. 97 (22 June 1981), pp. 22–24.

35. Ibid.

36. Robert Hotz, "Israeli Air Force Faces New Arab Arms," *Aviation Week & Space Technology*, Vol. 102 (10 March 1975), p. 14.

37. Harkavy, *Spectre of a Middle Eastern Holocaust*, p. 39.

38. Ibid., pp. 39–40.

39. Ibid., p. 40.

40. Smith, "U.S. Assumes the Israelis Have A-bomb or Its Parts," p. 8; Tahtinen, *The Arab-Israeli Military Balance Today*, p. 35.

41. "How Israel Got the Bomb," p. 39.

Conclusion

1. Robert E. Harkavy, *Spectre of a Middle Eastern Holocaust: The Strategic and Diplomatic Implications of the Israeli Nuclear Weapons Program* (Denver, CO: University of Denver for Monograph Series in World Affairs, 1977), p. 25.

2. Ibid., p. 26.

3. Steven J. Rosen, "Nuclearization and Stability in the Middle East," in *Nuclear Proliferation and the Near-Nuclear Countries*, ed. Onkar Marwah and Ann Schulz (Cambridge, MA: Ballinger Publishing Company, 1975), p. 157, passim; Shai Feldman, *Israeli Nuclear Deterrence: A Strategy for the 1980s* (New York: Columbia University Press, 1982), p. 242, passim.

4. Feldman, *Israeli Nuclear Deterrence*, p. 93.

5. Ibid.

6. Amos Natan, "Nuclear Arms: Solution or Despair?" in *Israel-Arab States: Atom Armed or Atom Free?* (Tel Aviv: Amikam Publishers, 1963), pp. 125–134 (cited in Ciro E. Zoppo, "The Nuclear Genie in the Middle East," *New Outlook*, Vol. 18 [February 1975], p. 24); Simha Flapan, "Nuclear Power in the Middle East" (Part 1), *New Outlook*, Vol. 17 (July 1974), p. 54; Yoram Nimrod and Amos Korczyn, "Suggested Patterns for Israeli-Egyptian Agreement to Avoid Nuclear Proliferation," *New Outlook*, Vol. 10 (January 1967), p. 9. Natan, Zoppo, Flapan, and Nimrod and Korczyn all agree with the conclusion that nuclear forces will destabilize the Middle East.

Bibliography

Books and Documents

Arms Trade and the Third World, The. New York: Humanities Press for Stockholm International Peace Research Institute, 1971.

Ashkar, Riad; Khalidi, Ahmed. *Weapons and Equipment of the Israeli Armed Forces.* Beirut, Lebanon: Institute for Palestine Studies, 1971.

Bader, William B. *The United States and the Spread of Nuclear Weapons.* New York: Pegasus for Center of International Studies, Princeton, 1968.

Barnaby, Frank; Goldblat, Jozef; Levinson, Macha. *The NPT: The Main Political Barrier to Nuclear Weapon Proliferation.* London and New York: Taylor & Francis and Crane, Russak & Company, for Stockholm International Peace Research Institute, 1980.

Beaton, Leonard. *Must the Bomb Spread?* Harmondsworth, U.K.: Penguin for The Institute for Strategic Studies, 1968.

Beaton, Leonard; Maddox, John. *The Spread of Nuclear Weapons.* New York: Praeger for the Institute for Strategic Studies, 1962.

Beckman, J. "Gas Centrifuges for Cheaper Isotope Separation." In *Preventing the Spread of Nuclear Weapons,* edited by C. F. Barnaby. London: Souvenir Press for Pugwash Movement, 1969.

Begin, Menachem. *The Revolt.* New York: Nash Publishing, 1977.

Ben-Gurion, David. *Israel: A Personal History.* New York: Funk and Wagnalls, 1971.

––––––. *Israel: Years of Challenge.* New York: Holt, Rinehart and Winston, 1963.

Beres, Louis René. *Apocalypse: Nuclear Catastrophe in World Politics.* Chicago and London: University of Chicago Press, 1980.

Bhatia, Shyam. *India's Nuclear Bomb.* Sahibabad, India: Vikas Publishing House, 1979.

Bonds, Ray (ed.). *The U.S. War Machine.* New York: Crown, 1983.

Červenka, Zdenek; Rogers, Barbara. *The Nuclear Axis: Secret Collaboration Between West Germany and South Africa.* New York: Times Books, 1978.

Committee for the Compilation of Materials on Damage Caused by the Atomic Bombs in Hiroshima and Nagasaki, The. *Hiroshima and Nagasaki.* Eisei Ishikawa and David L. Swain (translators). New York: Basic Books, 1981.

Crosbie, Sylvia K. *A Tacit Alliance: France and Israel from Suez to the Six Day War*. Princeton, NJ: Princeton University Press, 1974.

Davenport, Elaine; Eddy, Paul; Gillman, Peter. *The Plumbat Affair*. Philadelphia, PA: Lippincott, 1978.

Davidon, W.; Kalkstein, M.; Hohenemser, C. *The Nth Country Problem and Arms Control*. Washington, DC: National Planning Association, 1960.

De Volpi, Alexander. *Proliferation, Plutonium and Policy: Institutional and Technological Impediments to Nuclear Weapons Propagation*. New York: Pergamon Press, 1979.

Director of Military Survey, Tactical Pilotage Chart (United Kingdom: Ministry of Defense, 1981), Series TPC, Sheets G-4D, H-5A, Edition 2-GSGS.

Dornan, James E., Jr. "Tactical Nuclear Weapons and U.S. Military Capabilities." In *The U.S. War Machine*, edited by Ray Bonds. New York: Crown Publishers, 1983.

Dowty, Alan. "Israel: Perspective on Nuclear Proliferation." In *Security, Order, and the Bomb*, edited by Johan Jorgen Holst. Oslo: Oslo University Press, 1972.

Dunn, Lewis A. *Controlling the Bomb: Nuclear Proliferation in the 1980s*. New Haven and London: Yale University Press, 1982.

Dupuy, Trevor N.; Hayes, Grace P.; Andrews, John A. C. *The Almanac of World Military Power*. London and New York: R. R. Bowker, 1974.

Eban, Abba. *Abba Eban: An Autobiography*. New York: Random House, 1977.

Feldman, Shai. *Israeli Nuclear Deterrence: A Strategy for the 1980s*. New York: Columbia University Press, 1982.

Fisher, W. B. (ed.). *The Middle East and North Africa 1981–1982*. London: Europa Publications, 1981.

――――. *The Middle East and North Africa 1983–84*. London: Europa Publications, 1983.

Flapan, Simha. "Israel's Attitude Towards the NPT." In *Nuclear Proliferation Problems*, edited by Bhupendra Jasani. Cambridge, MA, London, Stockholm: MIT Press, Almqvist and Wiksell for SIPRI, 1974.

Gallois, Pierre. *The Balance of Terror*. Boston: Houghton-Mifflin, 1961.

Gervasi, Tom. *Arsenal of Democracy*. New York: Grove Press, 1981.

Glasstone, Samuel (ed.). *The Effects of Nuclear Weapons*. Washington, DC: GPO for U.S. Department of Defense and U.S. Atomic Energy Commission, 1962.

Goldschmidt, Bertrand. *The Atomic Adventure: Its Political and Technical Aspects*. London and New York: Pergamon Press and Macmillan Company, 1964.

Gunston, Bill. *An Illustrated Guide to Modern Fighters and Attack Aircraft*. New York: Arco, 1980.

Harkabi, Yehosafat. *Nuclear War and Nuclear Peace*. Yigal Shenkman (translator). Jerusalem: Israel Program for Scientific Translations, 1966.

Harkavy, Robert E. *Spectre of a Middle Eastern Holocaust: The Strategic and Diplomatic Implications of the Israeli Nuclear Weapons Program*.

Denver, CO: University of Denver for Monograph Series in World Affairs, 1977.

Haselkorn, Avigdor. "Israel: From an Option to a Bomb in the Basement?" In *Nuclear Proliferation: Phase II*, edited by R. M. Lawrence and J. Larus. Lawrence, KS: University of Kansas Press, 1974.

Heller, Mark; Tamari, Dov; Eytan, Zeev. *The Middle East Military Balance 1983*. Tel Aviv, Israel: *The Jerusalem Post* for Tel Aviv University and Jaffee Center for Strategic Studies, 1983.

Hersh, Seymour. *Chemical and Biological Warfare*. Garden City, NY: Doubleday, 1969.

Hohenemser, Christoph. "The Nth Country Problem Today." In *Disarmament: Its Politics and Economics*, edited by Seymour Melman. Boston: The American Academy of Arts and Sciences, 1962.

Holder, Simon. Personal correspondence (4 July 1983).

Hurewitz, J. C. *Middle East Politics: The Military Dimension*. New York: Praeger, 1969.

Jabber, Fuad. *Israel and Nuclear Weapons: Present Options and Future Strategies*. London: Chatto & Windus for The International Institute for Strategic Studies, 1971.

———. *Israel's Nuclear Option and U.S. Arms Control Policies*. Santa Monica, CA: California Arms Control and Foreign Policy Seminar, 1972.

Kemp, Geoffrey. *Arms and Security: The Egypt-Israel Case*. Adelphi Paper No. 52. London: The International Institute for Strategic Studies, 1968.

Ketzinel, Z. "Uranium Sources, Production and Demand in Israel." *Peaceful Uses of Atomic Energy*, Vol. 8 (New York and Vienna: United Nations and International Atomic Energy Agency, 1972).

Kramish, Arnold. *The Peaceful Atom in Foreign Policy*. New York: Harper & Row for the Council on Foreign Relations, 1963.

Lefever, Ernest W. *Nuclear Arms in the Third World: U.S. Policy Dilemma*. Washington, DC: The Brookings Institution, 1979.

London Sunday Times "Insight" Team. *The Yom Kippur War*. Garden City, NY: Doubleday, 1974.

Maddox, John. *Prospect for Nuclear Proliferation*. Adelphi Paper No. 113. London: The International Institute for Strategic Studies, 1975.

Mader, C. L. *Detonation Properties of Condensed Explosives*. Los Alamos: Los Alamos Scientific Laboratory, LA-2900, February 1963.

Mendl, Wolf. "The Spread of Nuclear Weapons: Lessons from the Past." In *Preventing the Spread of Nuclear Weapons*, edited by C. F. Barnaby. London: Souvenir Press for Pugwash Movement, 1969.

Military Balance 1981–1982, The. London: International Institute for Strategic Studies, 1981.

Military Balance 1983–1984, The. London: International Institute for Strategic Studies, 1983.

Natan, Amos. "Nuclear Arms: Solution or Despair?" In *Israel-Arab States: Atom Armed or Atom Free?* Tel Aviv: Amikam Publishers, 1963 (Hebrew).

Palit, D. K.; Namboodiri, P.K.S. *Pakistan's Islamic Bomb*. New Dehli: Vikas Publishing House, 1979.

Paxton, H. C. *Critical Dimensions of Systems Containing U-235, Pu-239, U-233.* Los Alamos: Los Alamos Scientific Laboratory, TID-7028, June 1964.

Perlmutter, Amos. *Military and Politics in Israel.* New York: Praeger, 1969.

Pranger, Robert J.; Tahtinen, Dale R. *Nuclear Threat in the Middle East.* Washington, DC: American Enterprise Institute for Public Policy Research, 1975.

Quester, George. Implications of SALT Outcome for Potential "Nth" Powers: Israel, India, and Others. Unpublished paper.

_____. "The Politics of Twenty Nuclear Powers." In *The Future of the International Strategic System,* edited by Richard Rosecrance. San Francisco: Chandler, 1972.

_____. *The Politics of Nuclear Proliferation.* Baltimore: Johns Hopkins University Press, 1973.

Report of the Secretary General (U Thant). *The Effects of the Possible Use of Nuclear Weapons and on the Security and Economic Implications for States of the Acquisition and Further Development of These Weapons.* New York: United Nations, Department of Political and Security Council Affairs, 1968.

Rosen, Steven J. "Nuclearization and Stability in the Middle East." In *Nuclear Proliferation and the Near-Nuclear Countries,* edited by Onkar Marwah and Ann Schulz. Cambridge, MA: Ballinger Publishing Company, 1975.

Rys, Steven L. *U.S. Military Power.* Greenwich, CT: Bison Books, 1983.

Tahtinen, Dale R. *The Arab-Israeli Military Balance Today.* Washington, DC: American Enterprise Institute for Public Policy Research, 1973.

_____. *The Arab-Israeli Military Balance Since October 1973.* Washington, DC: American Enterprise Institute for Public Policy Research, 1974.

Taylor, John W. R. (ed.). *Jane's All the World's Aircraft 1968–1969.* London: Jane's Publishing Company, 1968.

_____. *Jane's All the World's Aircraft 1980–1981.* London: Jane's Publishing Company, 1980.

_____. *Jane's All the World's Aircraft 1982–1983.* London: Jane's Publishing Company, 1982.

_____. *Jane's All the World's Aircraft 1983–1984.* London: Jane's Publishing Company, 1983.

Taylor, Theodore B. "Commerical Nuclear Technology and Nuclear Weapon Proliferation." In *Nuclear Proliferation and the Near-Nuclear Countries,* edited by Onkar Marwah and Ann Schulz. Cambridge, MA: Ballinger Publishing Company, 1975.

Tillotson, J. H. *Metallic Equations of State for Hypervelocity.* Gulf General Atomic, GA-3216.

Treaties and International Agreements Registered or Filed and Reported with the Secretariat of the United Nations. United Nations Treaty Series. Vol. 573, No. 8320.

U.S. Central Intelligence Agency. "Prospects for Further Proliferation of Nuclear Weapons" (memo dated 4 September 1974).

U.S. Congress, Joint Committee on Atomic Energy. *Nonproliferation of Nuclear Weapons.* Hearings on Senate Resolution 179. 89th Congress, 2nd Session, 1966.

U.S. Department of State. *United States Treaties and Other International Agreements.* Vol. 6, Pt. 2. Washington, DC: GPO, 1956.

_____. *United States Treaties and Other International Agreements.* Vol. 16, Pt. 2. Washington, DC: GPO, 1966.

U.S. *Department of State Bulletin.* Volume 44 (9 January 1961).

U.S. Disarmament and Arms Control Agency. "Report of Secretary General U Thant on the Effects of the Possible Use of Nuclear Weapons and on the Security and Economic Implications for States of the Acquisition and Further Development of These Weapons." In *Documents on Disarmament, 1967.* Washington, DC: GPO, 1968.

U.S. Foreign Policy and the Export of Nuclear Technology to the Middle East. Hearings before the Subcommittee on International Organizations and Movements and on the Near East and South Asia of the House Committee on Foreign Affairs. 93rd Congress, 2nd Session, 1974.

U.S. Office of Technology Assessment. *Nuclear Proliferation and Safeguards.* New York: Praeger, 1977.

Van Cleave, William. "Nuclear Technology and Weapons." In *Nuclear Proliferation: Phase II*, edited by R. M. Lawrence and J. Larus. Lawrence, KS: University of Kansas Press, 1974.

Weissman, Steve; Krosney, Herbert. *The Islamic Bomb.* New York: Times Books, 1981.

Willrich, Mason; Taylor, Theodore B. *Nuclear Theft: Risks and Safeguards.* Cambridge, MA: Ballinger Publishing Company, 1974.

World Armaments and Disarmament: SIPRI Yearbook 1977. Cambridge, MA, and London: MIT Press; Almqvist and Wiksell, 1977.

Articles

Alsop, Stewart; Lapp, Ralph. "Can the New A-Bomb Stop Troops in the Field?" *Saturday Evening Post,*, Vol. 224, Pt. 1 (29 September 1951).

"Atomic Artillery Tests," *Newsweek*, Vol. 38, Pt. 2 (22 October 1951).

"Baby Bombs," *Time,* Vol. 55, Pt. 2 (22 May 1950).

Barnaby, Frank. "The Continuing Body Count at Hiroshima and Nagasaki," *Bulletin of the Atomic Scientists,* Vol. 33 (December 1977).

Beaton, Leonard. "Nuclear Fuel-for-All," *Foreign Affairs,* Vol. 45 (July 1967).

_____. "Why Israel Does Not Need the Bomb," *New Middle East,* (April 1969).

Beecher, William. "Watch on Suez: Israel Weighs Options," *Army*, Vol. 21 (December 1971).

Begley, Sharon; Carey, John; Hall, Lynn. "How to Build a Bomb," *Newsweek,* Vol. 97 (22 June 1981).

Bell, J. Bowyer. "Israel's Nuclear Option," *The Middle East Journal,* Vol. 26 (Autumn 1972).

Ben-Tzur, Avraham. "The Arabs and the Israeli Reactor," *New Outlook* (March-April 1961).

Beres, Louis René. "Terrorism and the Nuclear Threat in the Middle East," *Current History*, Vol. 70–71 (January 1976).

"Big Ones & Little Ones," *Time*, Vol. 58, Pt. 2 (15 October 1951).

Committee for Nuclear Disarmament. "Keep Nuclear Weapons Out of Our Region," *New Outlook*, Vol. 9 (July-August 1966).

Deming, Angus; Kubic, Milan J.; Moreau, Ron. "Two Minutes over Baghdad," *Newsweek*, Vol. 97 (22 June 1981).

Evron, Yair. "Israel and the Atom: The Uses and Misuses of Ambiguity, 1957–1967," *Orbis*, Vol. 17 (Winter 1974).

Flapan, Simha. "Nuclear Power in the Middle East," (Part 1), *New Outlook*, Vol. 17, No. 6 (July 1974).

———. "Nuclear Power in the Middle East," (Part 2), *New Outlook*, Vol. 17, No. 8 (October 1974).

Freedman, Lawrence. "Israel's Nuclear Policy," *Survival*, Vol. 17 (May/June 1975).

Friedman, Todd. "Israel's Nuclear Option," *Bulletin of the Atomic Scientists*, Vol. 30 (September 1974).

Gillette, Robert. "Uranium Enrichment: Rumors of Israeli Progress with Lasers," *Science*, Vol. 183 (22 March 1974).

Gottlieb, Gidon. "Israel & The A-bomb," *Commentary*, Vol. 31 (February 1961).

Harkavy, Robert E. "The Pariah State Syndrome," *Orbis*, Vol. 21, No. 3 (Fall 1977).

Hodes, Aubrey. "Implications of Israel's Nuclear Capability," *The Wiener Library Bulletin*, Vol. 22 (Autumn 1968).

Hotz, Robert. "Israeli Air Force Faces New Arab Arms," *Aviation Week & Space Technology*, Vol. 102 (10 March 1975).

"How Israel Got the Bomb," *Time*, Vol. 107 (12 April 1976).

Jabber, Fuad. "Israel's Nuclear Intentions," *New Society* (11 November 1971).

———. "Not by War Alone: Curbing the Arab-Israeli Arms Race," *The Middle Eastern Journal*, Vol. 28 (Summer 1974).

Kohn, Howard; Newman, Barbara. "How Israel Got the Nuclear Bomb," *Rolling Stone*, No. 253 (1 December 1977).

Livneh, Eliezer. "Israel Must Come Out for Denuclearization," *New Outlook*, Vol. 9 (June 1966).

McElheny, Victor K. "The French Bomb: How Much Technical Fallout?" *Science*, Vol. 147 (1 January 1965).

Marcus, Joel. "The Rift Between Israel and France," *Midstream*, Vol. 14 (January 1968).

Morland, Howard. "The H-bomb Secret," *The Progressive*, Vol. 43 (November 1979).

Nimrod, Yoram; Korczyn, Amos. "Suggested Patterns for Israeli-Egyptian Agreement to Avoid Nuclear Proliferation," *New Outlook*, Vol. 10 (January 1967).

Norton, Augustus R. "Nuclear Terrorism and the Middle East," *Military Review,* Vol. 56 (April 1976).

Pa'il, Meir. "If a Nuclear Threat Should Become Part of the Arab-Israeli Conflict," *New Outlook,* Vol. 24-25 (May 1982).

Quester, George H. "Israel and the Nuclear Non-Proliferation Treaty," *Bulletin of the Atomic Scientists,* Vol. 25 (June 1969).

Robinson, Clarence A., Jr. "Lance Delivery to Israel Expected Soon," *Aviation Week & Space Technology,* Vol. 102 (17 February 1975).

Schlesinger, James R. "Nuclear Spread," *Yale Review,* Vol. 57 (Autumn 1967).

Strasser, Steven. "A Risky Nuclear Game," *Newsweek,* Vol. 97 (22 June 1981).

Szulc, Tad. "Murder by Proxy," *Penthouse* (August 1975).

"Tod aus der Textilfabrik," *Der Spiegel,* Vol. 23, No. 19 (5 May 1969).

Tucker, Robert W. "Israel and the United States: From Dependence to Nuclear Weapons?" *Commentary,* Vol. 60 (November 1975).

Valéry, Nicholas. "Israel's Silent Gamble with the Bomb," *New Scientist,* Vol. 64 (12 December 1974).

Y. V. "Atoms and a Middle East Tashkent," *New Outlook,* Vol. 9 (March-April 1966).

Willenson, Kim; Norman, Lloyd H.; Sullivan, Scott; and Kubic, Milan J. "Israel: A Friend in Need," *Newsweek* (12 September 1977).

Zoppo, Ciro E. "The Nuclear Genie in the Middle East," *New Outlook,* Vol. 18 (February 1975).

Newspaper Articles

Alsop, Joseph. "An Israeli Threat," *Washington Post* (7 October 1974).

Anderson, Jack. "3 Nations to Begin Cruise Missile Project," *Washington Post* (8 December 1980).

"Arafat Says Israel Has Nuclear Arms and Plans War," *New York Times* (4 April 1975).

"Article Says Israel Got C.I.A. Atomic Aid," *New York Times* (12 July 1975).

Beecher, William. "Israel Seen Holding 10 Nuclear Weapons," *Washington Post* (31 July 1975).

Berger, Marilyn. "Israeli Offers Vow on Use of A-Warheads," *Washington Post* (9 September 1975).

Binder, David. "C.I.A. Says Israel Has 10–20 A-Bombs," *New York Times* (16 March 1976).

———. "U.S. Finds Taiwan Develops A-Fuel," *New York Times* (30 August 1976).

Blaire, W. Granger. "France Explodes Her First A-Bomb in a Sahara Test," *New York Times* (13 February 1960).

"Bomb Called '45 Type," *New York Times* (8 November 1949).

"Bomb-Rich Uranium Reported Lost," *New York Times* (24 August 1977).

Braestrup, Peter. "France Will End Tests in Sahara," *New York Times* (16 March 1964).

Burnham, David. "Ex-C.I.A. Man Says Johnson Heard in '68 Israel Had A-Bombs," *New York Times* (2 March 1978).

Burns, John F. "Vorster Unequivocally Denies Nuclear Arms Program," *New York Times* (24 August 1977).

Burt, Richard. "Panel Doubts Flash Sighted Off Africa Was Atomic," *New York Times* (15 July 1980).

Butterfield, Fox. "Taiwan Denying Atomic Operation," *New York Times* (5 September 1976).

"Cairo Editor Says Israel Plans to Test Nuclear Device Soon," *New York Times* (21 August 1965).

Clarity, James F. "Teheran Denies Plans to Use Atom Plant for Nuclear Arms," *New York Times* (29 May 1976).

Cody, Edward. "Israel Angered as French Send Uranium to Iraq," *Washington Post* (20 July 1980).

Cohn, Victor. "Israel Says It Could Build Nuclear Weapons," *Washington Post* (3 December 1974).

"Dayan Bids U.S. Curb Mideast Arms Race," *New York Times* (26 August 1976).

"Dayan Says Israelis Have the Capacity to Produce A-Bombs," *New York Times* (25 June 1981).

Dulliforce, William. "Key Egyptian Urges Arabs Get or Make Atom Bomb," *Washington Post* (24 November 1973).

"Egypt to Get A-Bomb if Israel Explodes One," *Washington Post* (1 May 1976).

"Ex-C.I.A. Aide Says Johnson Quashed Israel A-Bomb Data," *Washington Post* (2 March 1978).

Feron, James. "Israelis Honor Atom Scientist," *New York Times* (14 May 1966).

Finney, John W. "U.S. Hears Israel Moves Toward A-Bomb Potential," *New York Times* (19 December 1960).

———. "U.S. Misled at First on Israeli Reactor," *New York Times* (20 December 1960).

———. "China Tests Atomic Bomb, Asks Summit Talk on Ban; Johnson Minimizes Peril," *New York Times* (17 October 1964).

Gerstenzang, James. Untitled, *New York Times* (19 October 1978), p. 5.

Getler, Michael. "A-Arms Believed in Egypt," *Washington Post* (21 November 1973).

Gillette, Robert. "U.S. Test Shows Nuclear Bombs Can Be Made from Low-Grade Plutonium," *Washington Post* (14 September 1977).

Giniger, Henry. "$16.7 Billion Military Program Is Approved by Paris Deputies," *New York Times* (10 October 1970).

Gruson, Sydney. "Wilson Proposes Nuclear-Free Zone in Mideast," *New York Times* (23 December 1964).

Halloran, Richard. "U.S. Holds off on Neutron Bomb; Some Officers Hail French Test," *New York Times* (28 June 1980).

Handler, M. S. "Adenauer to See Norstad Today in Preparation for Visit to U.S.," *New York Times* (21 May 1957).

Hill, Gladwin. "Cannon Fires Atomic Shell; Target 7 Miles Away Blasted," *New York Times* (26 May 1953).

Hoagland, Jim. "S. Africa, with U.S. Aid, near A-Bomb," *Washington Post* (16 February 1977).

———. "French Leader Confirms S. Africa Nuclear Ability," *Washington Post* (18 February 1977).

"Israel Bars U.S. Senators from A-Site," *Washington Post* (9 November 1976).

"Israel Believed Producing Missile of Atom Capability," *New York Times* (5 October 1971).

"Israel Denies a Report It Tested Atom Bomb in the South Atlantic," *New York Times* (23 February 1980).

"Israel Gets U.S. Atom Fuel," *New York Times* (4 March 1960).

"Israeli A-Bombs Put at 13," *Washington Post* (5 April 1976).

"Israeli Nuclear Deterrent Urged by Jerusalem Paper," *New York Times* (5 October 1968).

"Israeli Nukes," *Washington Post Parade Magazine* (12 April 1981).

"Israeli Publication Airs Nuclear Issue," *Washington Post* (12 June 1975).

"Israel Said Able to Make A-Bombs," *Washington Post* (12 October 1973).

"Israel Said to Plan to Make Atom Bomb," *New York Times* (14 June 1967).

Kramish, Arthur. "CIA: Israel Has 10–20 A-Weapons," *Washington Post* (15 March 1976).

Lewis, Flora. "France Said to Pledge to Replace Iraq-Bound Reactor," *New York Times* (9 May 1979).

McFadden, Robert D. "Rolling Stone Magazine Says Israelis Stole Uranium for Nuclear Arms," *New York Times* (25 October 1977).

Miller, Judith. "Senators Skeptical of Israeli Argument," *New York Times* (17 June 1981).

———. "3 Nations Widening Nuclear Contacts," *New York Times* (28 June 1981).

"Montreal Paper Asserts Israel Has Atomic Bombs," *New York Times* (8 May 1969).

"Nasser Threatens to War on a Nuclear-Armed Israel," *New York Times* (18 April 1966).

No Author. Untitled, *New York Times* (20 October 1978), p. 83.

"Nuclear Missile Trucks Shown at Bastille Day Parade," *New York Times* (15 July 1970).

O'Toole, Thomas. "Earlier Try of Indian Bomb Told," *Washington Post* (13 July 1974).

———. "Magazine Says Israelis Hijacked A-Bomb Fuel," *Washington Post* (25 October 1977).

———. "Lost Uranium Mystery," *Washington Post* (6 November 1977).

———. "Making Plutonium Held Easier Than Supposed," *Washington Post* (10 November 1977).

———. "CIA Repeats Fears on Missing Uranium," *Washington Post* (28 February 1978).

O'Toole, Thomas; Berger, Marilyn. "Tiniest A-Blasts Identifiable Now," *Washington Post* (11 April 1971).

"Paper Says Israel Has 10 Atom Bombs," *New York Times* (1 August 1975).

"Paris Announces Improved A-Bombs," *New York Times* (13 July 1965).

"Peking Is Upgraded on Atom Technique," *New York Times* (22 October 1964).

"Possible Role of Mideast Agents in Toulon Reactor Blast Study," *New York Times* (14 April 1979).

Shapley, Deborah. "CIA Report Says Israel Secretly Obtained A-Matter," *Washington Post* (28 January 1978).

Shipler, David K. "Israel Bans a Book on Atomic 'Arsenal,' " *New York Times* (30 March 1980).

———. "Israelis Are Critical of U.S. Decision to Hold Up F-16s for Raid on Iraq," *New York Times* (12 June 1981).

Smith, Hedrick. "Ulbricht Visit to Cairo Today Said to Have Been Urged by Soviet," *New York Times* (24 February 1965).

———. "Warning on Bomb Given by Nasser," *New York Times* (21 February 1966).

———. "U.S. Assumes the Israelis Have A-Bomb or Its Parts," *New York Times* (18 July 1970).

Smith, Terence. "Jet Crash-Lands," *New York Times* (22 February 1973).

"South Africa Link to Israel Grows," *New York Times* (18 August 1976).

"South Africa Says It Is Not Planning Atomic Bomb Tests," *New York Times* (22 August 1977).

"Soviet Said to Give Arabs Atom Pledge," *New York Times* (14 December 1974).

Sulzberger, C. L. "Foreign Affairs," *New York Times* (16 November 1963).

"Taipei Denies Work on Atomic Weapons," *New York Times* (8 July 1975).

Tanner, Henry. "French Hint Plan to Build ICBMs," *New York Times* (28 February 1968).

Teltsch, Kathleen. "Egyptian at the U.N. Accuses Israelis of 'Nuclear Collusion' with South Africa and of Threatening Peace," *New York Times* (1 June 1978).

"U.N. Panel Surveys Israeli Atom Skill," *New York Times* (9 July 1981).

"U.S. Doubts Israel Set Off A-Bomb," *New York Times* (22 February 1980).

Uya, Stanley, "Israel Held Giving South Africa Military Information," *Washington Post* (8 July 1975).

"Vorster Unequivocally Denies Nuclear Arms Program," *New York Times* (24 August 1977).

Walz, Jay. "Nasser Exhibits Military Might," *New York Times* (24 July 1962).

Weinraub, Bernard. "India Becomes 6th Nation to Set Off Nuclear Device," *New York Times* (19 May 1974).

Wilson, George C. "Nuclear War Feared Next Time in Mideast," *Washington Post* (13 July 1975).

Index

DATE DUE

MAY 0 4 1988			
NOV 2 2 2000			